Should I Retire Now?

A Practical, No-Nonsense Guide to Making the Retirement Decision and Landing on Your Feet

Ayson R. Boone

Latitude 16 Degrees Press

This book is a work of nonfiction. While it draws on general experiences common to many people approaching or entering retirement, all anecdotes, names, examples, and characters are fictionalized, generalized, or used illustratively unless explicitly stated. Any resemblance to actual persons, living or deceased, is purely coincidental.

Interior images generated using ChatGPT and selected by the author.

Published by Latitude 16 Degrees Press
An imprint of Latitude 16 Degrees
ISBN: 978-1-923820-00-5 – ebook
ISBN: 978-1-923820-01-2 – paperback
Print editions are produced and distributed through print-on-demand and publishing distribution partners.

First Edition

AI Use Declaration

This book was conceived, directed, written, and edited by the author. Some interior images were generated using ChatGPT. Generative AI tools were also used to support brainstorming, editing, proofreading, and wording refinement. The author reviewed, revised, selected, and approved the final content. The author remains responsible for the content of this book, including its accuracy, interpretation, tone, citations, and final presentation.

Reader Responsibility Disclaimer

This book is intended for general information, reflection, and educational purposes only. It is not financial, legal, medical, psychological, tax, employment, pension, retirement, or superannuation advice. Readers are responsible for how they interpret and use the material, and for any decisions or actions they take as a result. Before making significant decisions, seek advice from appropriately qualified professionals who understand your personal circumstances.

Dedication

To everyone who has ever cried in a workplace car park and knew it was time.

And to Roger — who stood beside me through every doubt, detour, and decision on the road to retirement. You were the calm in my storm, the steady voice of reason when I lost mine, and the one who never said "I told you so," even when you probably should have. Thank you for holding the space, the hope, and the wine — and for quietly reminding me that life could be more than work.

How to Use this Book

This book is designed for the decision stage of retirement. Its job is not to hand you a perfect answer, a perfect financial plan, or a perfect vision of your future self wearing linen beside a tasteful herb garden. Its job is to help you think clearly about whether to leave, linger, or lighten the load, and what you need to consider before that decision becomes real.

It is not a financial planning manual. It will not tell you where to invest, how to structure your pension or superannuation, or whether you should buy a yacht and call it "Tax Deduction." Please do not do that on the basis of this book. Retirement money decisions can have long-term consequences, so seek qualified advice about your own circumstances before making major financial, legal, tax, pension, or superannuation decisions.

You do not have to read this book in order. You can read from beginning to end, or you can start with the chapter that matches the thing currently keeping you awake. If money is shouting the loudest, go to Chapter 5. If your body is sending warning signals, start with Chapter 2. If retirement has happened to you before you were ready, Chapter 4 may be the place to begin. The book is structured as a pathway, but you are allowed to enter through whichever door is already open.

At the end of each chapter, you will find three short sections: **What To Take With You**, **Questions Worth Asking**, and **Try This Before You Move On**. These are not tests. Nobody is assessing your performance. There is no bonus, promotion, or neatly framed certificate waiting at the end. They are there to help you turn the chapter from something you have read into something you can use.

What To Take With You summarize the main points, especially if your brain is tired and has started retaining information like a sieve with commitment issues. **Questions Worth Asking** are there to slow the panic loop. They help you name what is actually going on, rather than letting the whole decision float around as one large, shapeless dread-cloud. **Try This Before You Move On** are small action steps. They are designed to move the question out of your head and onto paper, where it usually becomes less dramatic and more useful. You can do them in a notebook, on your computer, on scrap paper, or on the back of an envelope while muttering darkly into a cup of tea. The method matters less than the honesty.

You do not need to complete every exercise immediately. Some chapters may only need a quick read. Others may ask you to stop, think, write things down, or have a conversation you have been avoiding. If an exercise feels too much, leave it for now and come back to it. Avoidance is not the goal, but neither is emotional weightlifting before breakfast.

You are not trying to solve the rest of your life in one sitting. You are trying to decide what comes next. The chapter tools are there to help you do that one question, one page, and one practical step at a time.

Contents

Introduction

I spent nearly three decades in academia before I finally admitted what my body had been trying to tell me for at least the last two years — I was done. Not in a dramatic, hand-in-my-resignation-and-storm-out kind of way. More in a quiet, bone-deep exhaustion that no amount of annual leave could fix. The decision to retire was not a triumphant reinvention. It was a sensible choice made in the name of health, sanity, and a future that seemed livable.

Did the prospect of retiring feel intimidating? Of course it did. That did not surprise me. What surprised me most was that so much of the advice I found seemed to assume the choice had already been made. There was plenty of the usual talk about golf, gardening, travel, and finally learning Italian, as well as the serious business of financial planning and working out whether you could afford to stop. There was far less guidance about how to actually make that choice when you are tired, coming apart at the seams, and your mind is running faster than your ability to cope.

I looked for a book that would help me get through this transition nobody warns you about, the money panic that shows up at three in the morning, the self-doubt, the second-guessing, the exhaustion that makes every decision feel heavier than it should. I also wanted a book that acknowledged involuntary retirement situations, such as redundancy, health crises, workplace restructures, as real and common, rather than shameful exceptions to the glossy brochure version of retirement.

I didn't find that book. So, I wrote it.

This book is for the person who is running out of fuel but is not sure whether stopping work is wise, possible, or even safe. It is for the person who has always pushed through but is now wondering whether pushing through is sustainable or just slow-motion self-harm.

It is for anyone facing burnout, a wake-up call about their health, a workplace restructure, or the quiet realization that work is costing them more than it is giving back.

You will not find motivational fluff here. No platitudes on finding your passion or reinventing yourself by Thursday. No lectures about having a perfect financial plan before you are allowed to consider retirement. What you will find is a practical, honest guide to making the call, preparing for the transition, and landing with a little more steadiness and a lot less panic.

Retirement is not a single event. It is a decision, a transition, and a landing. This book is meant to help you navigate all three.

You do not need to have everything figured out before you begin. You just need to start.

And, this is a good place to begin.

Chapter 1

So, You Are Thinking About Retirement — Now What?

Jasmine had not planned to think seriously about retirement until at least next year. Then, within the same month, she turned sixty, sat through yet another workplace "change proposal" briefing, which seemed suspiciously like a planned restructure, and ended up crying in the car after a meeting that should not have been a big deal but somehow was. Suddenly, retirement was no longer a vague future concept involving a linen pantsuit and better coffee. It felt close enough to touch, and just far enough away to be terrifying.

If you have picked up this book, you may be in a version of that same moment. Maybe you woke up one day and realized you could not face another year. Maybe your body started sending louder signals. Maybe redundancy arrived uninvited, or a health scare made the decision feel less optional. Or maybe you are simply tired in a way sleep no longer fixes, and the question Should I retire now? has moved from idle daydream to something that needs an actual answer.

That shift from "someday" to "possibly now" can feel enormous. This chapter is about that moment: why it suddenly feels so real, why it can feel so urgent, and why retirement often looks less like one clear emotion and more like a jumble of promise, dread, and paperwork.

Why This Suddenly Feels Very Real

For most of your working life, retirement probably sat somewhere in the category of "things I will think about later," alongside decluttering the spare bedroom and learning to play the drums. It was a vague, distant concept that belonged to other people, the ones with sensible hobbies and a clear sense of what they wanted to do with their time.

Then something changed.

Maybe it was a birthday that carried more weight than the ones before it. Maybe it was a workplace restructure that made you realize your job security was more fragile than you had assumed. Maybe it was a health scare, yours or someone close to you, that reminded you time is not infinite, and bodies do not wait for convenient moments to send warnings. Maybe it was simply the accumulation of too many bad weeks in a row, until you could no longer tell yourself it was just a rough patch.

Whatever the trigger, retirement has moved from theoretical to real. And that shift can feel enormous.

The Triggers That Make Retirement Real

Research on retirement decision-making suggests that the move from "someday" to "possibly now" is often shaped by a mix of personal, health, work, family, and financial factors rather than one calm, perfectly timed moment of readiness.[1] These triggers often arrive close together, which is part of why the decision can suddenly feel so urgent. In real life, people rarely sit down with a cup of tea and calmly announce, *"Ah yes, this is the precise psychological, financial, and logistical moment to retire."* More often, a mix of events, reminders, and changing circumstances brings the question into view, making retirement feel like an option worth considering. Some of the most common triggers include:

Age milestones can carry surprising weight. Turning sixty, or sixty-five, or whatever age makes retirement suddenly feel less hypothetical, can shift the whole question from distant possibility to immediate option. Even if nothing else has changed, the number itself can make the question harder to ignore.

Workplace changes can also bring the retirement question closer. Restructures, new management, policy modifications, or the quiet realization that your workplace no longer values what you bring can make staying feel less sustainable. Sometimes it is not a single dramatic event but a steady erosion of goodwill, energy, and patience.

Health events are perhaps the most visceral trigger. A diagnosis, a new medication, a conversation with a doctor that includes the phrase "you need to reduce your stress". It is these moments that can make retirement seem less like a lifestyle choice and more like a survival strategy.

Fatigue is harder to name but just as real. Not the kind of tiredness that a weekend fixes, but the kind that has seeped into your bones and refuses to move along. The kind that makes you wonder whether you have another year left in you, let alone five.

Social cues matter too. When colleagues start retiring, when friends begin talking about their plans, when your peer group shifts from "we will retire someday" to "I am seriously thinking about it," retirement stops being abstract and starts feeling like something you are allowed to consider.

Why This Feels So Urgent

Part of what makes this moment seem so intense is that retirement is not just one decision. It is several decisions stacked on top of each other, all calling for attention at once.

Can you afford it?

Should you go now or wait?

What will you do with your time?

Who will you be without your job?

What if you regret it?

These questions do not arrive politely, one at a time. They arrive in a rush, often when you are already tired and least equipped to think clearly. And because retirement feels irreversible, even though it is not always, the stakes can feel impossibly high.

The other reason this moment can feel so urgent is that it may coincide with a loss of control. If you are being pushed out, or your health is declining, or your energy has run out, the decision may no longer feel entirely yours. Retirement starts to feel as though it is arriving whether you feel ready or not, and that can make the fear louder.

From Panic to Clarity

For Jasmine, that was the first real shift. She had not answered the question yet, but she stopped pretending it was just a passing mood. Once she admitted the question was real, it became a little less frightening and a lot more workable. If retirement has suddenly become real for you, the first thing to know is this — you do not need to have all the answers right now. You do not need to make the decision today. You do not need to pretend you are calm when you are not.

What you need is a way to move from panic to clarity. A way to sort through the questions, separate the urgent from the optional, and work out what actually matters. That is what the rest of this book will help you do.

Retirement – Dream, Threat, or Mild Administrative Crisis?

Retirement occupies a strange psychological space. For some people, it looks like a dream: freedom from meetings, no more performance reviews, sleeping past six-thirty without guilt. For others, it feels like a threat: loss of income, loss of identity, loss of the structure that has held life together for decades. And for a surprising number of people, it lands somewhere in the middle: a mildly administrative crisis involving paperwork, phone calls to check on your retirement savings, pension, or superannuation accounts, depending on where you are in the world, and the vague sense that you are supposed to be doing something important but cannot quite remember what. The truth is, retirement is rarely just one of these things. It is often all three at once, sometimes before lunch.

The Dream Version

The dream version of retirement is seductive. No alarm clocks. No commute. No workplace politics. Time to read, travel, garden, or finally learn Italian. Time to do all the things you have been putting off for thirty years because work got in the way.

This version is not entirely fantasy. Retirement can deliver freedom, rest, and the chance to reclaim your time. Research on retirement adjustment suggests that people tend to fare better when retirement is voluntary, resourced, and supported by enough preparation to make the transition manageable.[1, 2] For some people, that relief is real. But it is not the whole story.

The dream version tends to skip over the awkward bits — the identity wobble when you no longer have a job title, the flatness that can arrive even when you thought you would feel excited, as well as the quiet panic that shows up when you realize you have no idea what to do with a Tuesday.

The Threat Version

For others, retirement feels less like freedom and more like falling off a cliff. The threat version is louder, more visceral, and harder to dismiss. What if you run out of money? What if you become irrelevant? What if you lose your sense of purpose and spend the rest of your life drifting?

These fears are not irrational. Retirement can involve real uncertainties — money, social connection, daily structure, and the loss of a work role that may have carried more identity than you realized.[1, 2] Those uncertainties can make the threat version feel very real.

Research on retirement adjustment suggests that the conditions under which people leave work matter. Retirement tends to be easier to adjust to when it feels chosen and resourced, and harder when it is shaped by poor health, pressure, job loss, or limited control.[3, 4] When retirement happens to you rather than being chosen by you, the threat version feels very real.

Even voluntary retirement can feel threatening if you have not prepared emotionally or practically. Leaving work without some sense of what comes next can leave you feeling untethered, anxious, and uncomfortably aware that you have just walked away from the thing that organized your entire adult life.

The Mild Administrative Crisis Version

And then there is the version nobody warns you about — retirement as a series of tedious, mildly confusing tasks that need doing before you can actually relax.

Updating your pension or retirement fund details. Working out your tax situation. Sorting health insurance. Transferring files off your work laptop. Cleaning out your office. Telling people. Filling in forms. Waiting on hold with government departments while slowly losing faith in humanity. This version is not dramatic. It is just annoying. And surprisingly time-consuming.

One recently retired teacher described her first month as "less freedom, more admin". She had imagined sleeping in and reading novels. Instead, she spent three weeks chasing paperwork, attending exit meetings, and trying to work out whether her leave entitlements had been paid correctly.

The administrative version is the least emotionally charged, but it is also the most underestimated. People prepare for the big emotional shifts in things like freedom, loss, and identity, but forget that retirement also involves a dozen small practical jobs that nobody explains in advance.

Which Version Is Yours?

The answer is probably all of them, at different times.

Retirement is not a single experience. Research on retirement adjustment describes it as a process rather than a one-time event.[1, 2] In real life, that means it can unfold over months, sometimes years, and contain more than one emotion at the same time. You can feel relieved and terrified in the same week. You can enjoy your freedom and still grieve what you have lost. You can be genuinely glad you left and still wonder if you made a mistake.

What matters is not which version you are experiencing right now. What matters is that you have a way to navigate all three without pretending any of them are invalid.

So...Here You Are

By this point, retirement is no longer a vague future concept reserved for other people with better pensions or retirement savings and more enthusiasm for gardening. It has become a live question in your own life. Maybe it showed up quietly. Maybe it barged in wearing steel-capped boots. Either way, it is here now, and it wants your attention.

That alone can feel unsettling. Once the question becomes real, it has a way of coloring everything else — work, health, money, energy, identity, even how much patience you have left for strategic planning meetings and cheerful emails marked "gentle reminder."

You Are Not Behind

You might not have all the answers yet. You might not even know what the right questions are. But you have already done something important. You have stopped brushing this off as a vague someday issue and acknowledged that it matters.

That is not a small thing.

Retirement is a major life transition, and many people are expected to work it out with very little preparation and even less honest conversation. Many people stumble into it carrying a jumble of hope, fear, relief, denial, and a folder full of paperwork they do not entirely understand. You are not behind because you do not feel clear yet. You are normal.

You are also further along than you think. The moment you stop pretending and start paying attention, you are already doing the real work of this transition.

Where This Leaves You

Before we get to plans, numbers, and practicalities, we need to sort feeling from fact. Not every difficult season means it is time to retire. But not every act of endurance is wisdom, either.

The temptation now is to demand certainty, to skip ahead to the part where someone sensible hands you a neat framework, a reliable timeline, and a crisp answer to the question: *Should I retire now?*

Before you can answer that question, you need to understand what is driving it. Is this a bad patch? A body asking for a different pace? A workplace that has become too draining to endure? Or a genuine sign that it may be time to stop, or at least stop pretending that you can keep going exactly as you are?

Jasmine still did not know whether she would retire now, later, or by some middle path. But she knew this much — the question had earned its place on the table, and she was allowed to take it seriously.

For now, you do not need a final answer. You just need to recognize that the question is real, that something has shifted, and that paying attention is a valid place to begin.

That is where the next chapter begins.

What to Take With You

Retirement often becomes real not because of one dramatic moment, but because something specific pushes the question forward. That trigger can be any number of things: health, fatigue, age, workplace change, or sheer depletion. Suddenly, "someday" starts to feel like "possibly now."

It is normal for retirement to feel like a dream, a threat, and a mildly administrative crisis all at once.

At this stage, you do not need a final answer. You need to recognize what is making the question feel urgent and begin sorting panic from reality.

Questions Worth Asking

What has made retirement feel more real to me lately — health, exhaustion, workplace changes, age, finances, or something else?

When I think about retirement right now, does it feel more like freedom, fear, or overwhelm — and what might that be telling me?

Try This Before You Move On – The Triggers Check

Take a sheet of paper and write down the following question: *"Why is retirement on my mind now?"*

Next, list the specific triggers that have brought you to this point. These might include a health event, ongoing fatigue, a birthday, workplace change, financial pressure, caring responsibilities, or simply the feeling that you cannot keep doing this indefinitely. Put a star next to the one that feels most significant. Then write two or three sentences about why that trigger matters now.

Chapter 2

Should I Retire Now? How to Know When It's Time (and When It's Not)

Leah sat in her car outside work with the engine off and her hands still gripping the steering wheel. She was not crying exactly, but she was close enough to see it as a warning. Lately, everything felt harder than it should — getting up, getting through the day, pretending she still cared. She was tired in a way a weekend did not fix, flat in a way coffee did not touch, and increasingly unsure whether "just keep going" was wisdom or self-neglect. For the first time, she allowed herself to ask a question she had been dodging for months — *what if it really was time to go?*

The question had been building for months, maybe longer. Not loudly. Not dramatically. Just a persistent hum beneath everything else — *Is it time?* And then, more urgently — *How do I know?*

This chapter is about recognizing the signs that work is no longer sustainable and learning to tell the difference between a bad patch and something more serious. Because not every rough week means you should hand in your resignation. But not every "just push through" is wise either. And the gap between those two realities is where most people get stuck.

Some of the signs are obvious. They show up in your body — the sleep that will not come, the exhaustion that a weekend cannot fix, the sense that you are running on fumes and have been for longer than you care to admit. Other signs are quieter and harder to name.

The flatness. The irritability. The dread on Sunday evenings. The tears in the car park. The fantasy of walking out mid-meeting and never coming back.

None of these signs means you are weak. They mean you are human, and that something important has shifted.

The trouble is that most of us have spent decades learning to override these signals. We have been trained to push through, to be resilient, to prove we can handle it. And for a long time, maybe we could. But burnout does not care how capable you used to be. It cares how much you have left.

When work is no longer sustainable, the strain rarely stays neatly at work. For the purposes of this chapter, we will look for it in four places: the body, the mind, the work itself, and home life. And if the signs are appearing across all four, the question is no longer whether you are tough enough to keep going. The question is whether continuing is wise, safe, or sustainable.

This chapter will help you work out whether the question has become serious enough to require a decision. The framework for making that decision is presented in the next chapter. Here, the goal is simpler — to identify the signs, take them seriously, and distinguish a difficult season from something more fundamental. We will do that by looking at the four places work strain usually leaves its mark — body, mind, work, and home life.

Let's start with the signs.

The Car Park Cry Test: When Work Stops Being Annoying and Starts Being Damaging

There is a moment many people recognize, but few talk about openly. You finish your workday, walk to your car, sit down, close the door, and suddenly the tears come. Not because something catastrophic happened. Not because anyone was cruel. Just because you are so profoundly tired that the simple act of getting through another day has left you empty. Or it happens in reverse — you arrive in the car park in the morning, sit there with your hands on the wheel, and think, *I just cannot do this today,* and then the tears come.

I call this the **Car Park Cry Test**. And if you have experienced it more than once, it is worth paying attention.

The Car Park Cry Test is not about having a bad day. Everyone has bad days. It is about the point where frustrating meetings, tedious admin, a million things to do, and difficult colleagues stop being merely annoying and start being damaging. It is the moment your body and mind are trying to tell you something important: this is no longer sustainable.

One way to understand this is through the idea of depletion. In a well-known "radish experiment," hungry students were placed in a room with freshly baked cookies and radishes. Some were told they could eat the cookies. Others were told they could only eat the radishes. Afterward, both groups were given an impossible puzzle to solve. The radish-eaters gave up after an average of eight minutes, while the cookie-eaters persisted for nearly twenty minutes.[5] The difference was not character. It was depletion. The students who had to resist the cookies had already used up part of their self-control reserves before they even reached the puzzle.

Work can feel like that too. When you spend all day managing difficult situations, suppressing frustration, meeting impossible demands, and pretending you are fine, it is not surprising that you feel drained by the end of the day.

Of course, not every tear in a car park can be explained by one experiment. The point is that sustained effort, self-control, and emotional containment can leave you with far less capacity than you started with. By the time you reach your car, there may be very little left to give. The tears are not a sign of weakness. They are a sign of depletion. And if the tears come before work, they may be telling you something just as important — you are no longer walking into the day with steadiness but bracing yourself against it.

Fumio Sasaki describes a familiar version of this in *Hello, Habits*:

> If we continue to work overtime at work, we stop by a convenience store on our way home and buy sweets or drink lots of alcohol. In that state, we get short-tempered over the smallest actions by someone else.[6]

In other words, when people are worn down by chronic overwork, they reach for quick comforts, lose patience more easily, and find even small demands harder to absorb. At some point, rest becomes necessary and stops being optional.

How the Signs of Work Strain First Show Up

Research indicates that chronic work stress can contribute to burnout and affect both mental and physical health.[7, 8] But in real life, the warning signs do not usually arrive as one neat announcement that something has gone wrong. The signs of damage, rather than simple annoyance, often show up first as symptoms. For the purposes of this chapter, it helps to sort the signs into four rough groups: physiological, emotional, behavioral, and cognitive.

- **Physiological symptoms** might include headaches or backaches, digestive changes, dizziness or nausea, muscle tension, lowered immunity, raised blood pressure, poor sleep, or the kind of tiredness that rest does not fix.
- **Emotional symptoms** can look like feeling hopeless, dread, flatness, feelings of guilt when at rest, irritability, numbness, loss of motivation, or crying in the car.
- **Behavioral symptoms** often show up in what starts slipping like withdrawing from people, reaching for quick comforts (for example, consuming higher amounts of drugs, alcohol, food, or sugar), neglecting exercise or hobbies, trouble getting out of bed, or spending your weekends recovering rather than living.
- **Cognitive symptoms** can include brain fog, forgetfulness, poor concentration, cynicism or negative thinking, indecision, and the sense that even simple tasks now take more effort than they should.

In real life, these signs rarely stay neatly in one category. A tired body can affect your mood. A difficult workplace can follow you home. A change at home can make work feel harder than it used to. For this chapter, we will track them across four areas of life: body, mind, work, and home life:

- **Body:** sleep that will not come, sleep you cannot wake from, persistent tiredness that sleep does not resolve, increased susceptibility to colds and infections, changes in appetite, weight, or digestion without a clear cause, blood pressure creeping up, tension headaches that arrive on schedule, frequent headaches, muscle tension, and exhaustion that weekends no longer fix.

- **Mind:** feeling flat, numb, unusually detached, irritable, foggy, forgetful, unable to concentrate, unable to make decisions, or as though everything requires more effort than it should.

- **Work:** dreading the workday, shutting down before it begins, struggling to complete tasks that were once straightforward, losing interest in work that used to matter, or feeling as though you are pushing through rather than functioning well.

- **Home life:** crying in the car, irritability spilling into home life, withdrawing from friends or family, avoiding people, reaching for alcohol, junk food, or online shopping because you have no energy left for better choices, letting exercise, hobbies, and self-care slide, and spending your non-work hours recovering rather than living.

These are not signs that you are weak. They are signs that you are human, and that something has changed.

The question is not whether you are tough enough to keep going. The question is whether continuing is safe. And if the answer is no — or even maybe — then it is time to stop dismissing the car park tears as dramatics and start treating them as data.

Leah was facing an impossible workload, and financial strain made the choice feel even harder. When getting through the day starts to feel like survival, work may have crossed the line from annoying to damaging.

If you have cried in your car more than once in recent months, you do not need to justify it. You need to listen to it. Your body is trying to tell you something. The only question left is whether you are ready to hear it.

Reading the Signals: Burnout, Boredom, and the Body's Quiet Protest

As Leah read through the signs, she realized the tears in the car and the bone-deep fatigue were not isolated incidents. They belonged to a pattern. What had seemed vague and slightly embarrassing started to look more like information.

Not all exhaustion looks the same. Sometimes it arrives with sirens — a health crisis, a breakdown, a moment so dramatic you cannot ignore it. But more often, it creeps in quietly. A little slower to recover each week. A little less patience for things that used to roll off your back. A little more effort is required to care about work that once mattered. Burnout often builds gradually, which is one reason people can miss the early signs.[7, 9] This is the body's quiet protest. And if you have been ignoring it, you are not alone.

Burnout is not simply feeling tired. The World Health Organization describes it as an occupational phenomenon resulting from chronic workplace stress that has not been successfully managed.[10] It is usually understood through three dimensions: exhaustion or energy depletion, depersonalization — a kind of mental distance or cynical detachment from work, and reduced personal accomplishment or efficacy.[9, 10] In plain English, burnout is what happens when the relationship between you and your work has been strained for too long.

What makes burnout particularly insidious is that capable people can be very good at explaining it away. You have spent decades proving you can handle pressure. You have pushed through before. You have been resilient. So, when the signs start showing up, you dismiss them as temporary. A bad patch. Something a holiday will fix.

Except it doesn't. And the signals get louder.

Christina Maslach, whose work helped establish burnout as a major area of workplace research, emphasizes that burnout is tied to the relationship between the person and the job, not simply to individual weakness.[9] It is not about lacking resilience. It is about working in conditions that deplete you faster than you can recover.

So, when the earlier signs begin clustering — the emotional exhaustion, the detachment and numbness, the ineffectiveness and self-doubt, the tears, the fog, the self-care slippage

— the question is not whether you are being dramatic. The question is whether your current way of working is still sustainable.

Boredom, too, is a signal worth heeding. Not the occasional *this meeting could have been an email* boredom, but the deeper kind — the sense that your work no longer challenges or engages you. You feel detached from your work as if you are just going through motions without meaning. Chronic boredom at work has been linked with poorer work-related wellbeing, including lower job satisfaction and stronger intentions to leave.[11] Sometimes boredom is a sign that you have outgrown your role.

Sometimes boredom is a sign that the work itself has changed in ways that no longer suit you. And sometimes it is your mind's way of telling you that you have given enough, and it is time to direct your energy elsewhere.

The question is not whether those signals are dramatic enough to justify action. The question is whether you are listening. Because your body is not trying to be dramatic. It is trying to get your attention, in the only language it has, when something no longer feels sustainable.

If you have been dismissing those signals as weaknesses, it is time to reframe them as data. Useful, important, self-preserving data. The kind that helps you make decisions before your body makes them for you.

Why It May Be Time to Go and Why That Does Not Mean You Failed

Somewhere along the way, many of us absorbed the idea that leaving a job before we absolutely had to, before retirement age, before being forced out, before our bodies gave up entirely, meant we had fallen short. That we were not tough enough. Not resilient enough. Not committed enough.

This belief is nonsense, but it is remarkably persistent nonsense.

Choosing to retire because you are exhausted, because your health is suffering, because the job has changed in ways that no longer suit you, or because you have simply had enough is not a personal failing. It is self-preservation. It is wisdom. It is recognizing that your energy, health, and time are finite resources, and deciding to use them differently.

Research on occupational health links prolonged job strain with serious health risks, including cardiovascular disease.[12] Staying in a damaging job does not make you strong. It makes you vulnerable. And leaving before the damage becomes harder to reverse is not a sign of weakness. It is strategy.

Yet the guilt persists. Particularly for high-functioning people who have spent decades proving their capability, the notion of stepping back can feel like you are admitting defeat. You worry about what colleagues will think. What your family will say. Whether you are letting people down. Whether you are giving up too easily.

Let's be clear. If you have been working for twenty, thirty, or forty years, you have not given up easily. You have given plenty. And recognizing that you have given enough is not the same as quitting.

There is also the question of identity. For many people, work has been the primary organizer of life — the thing that gave structure, status, purpose, and a ready answer to the question, *What do you do?* Stepping away from that can feel like losing a part of yourself. And in some ways, it is.

But it is also making space for something else – something quieter, slower, and harder to name, but no less valuable. This is a textbook case of "role exit", a concept popularized in 1988 by sociologist Helen Rose Fuchs Ebaugh, who described it as the process of disengaging from a role that has been central to identity and building a new sense of self outside of it.[13] That may sound tidy, but in practice, letting go of a familiar role can feel anything but tidy.

Retirement researcher Nancy Schlossberg frames retirement as part of a larger pattern of life transitions — the ongoing process of moving out of one location, relationship, job, career, or role and into another. [14] In real life, though, the "out of" part often becomes clear before the "into" part does. That is what makes the in-between stage feel so uncomfortable.

Transitions require you to loosen your grip on what was, often before you have any clear idea of what comes next. And that in-between stage can feel deeply uncomfortable.

The other thing worth naming is this — sometimes the decision to retire is not really a choice. Sometimes it is forced by redundancy, illness, caregiving responsibilities, or workplace conditions that have become untenable. And if that is your situation, the guilt can be even sharper. You did not get to leave on your terms. You did not get the farewell you imagined. You did not get to finish strong.

But here is the truth. An unplanned exit is not a lesser exit. It is an exit that happened differently than you expected. And while that brings its own grief and adjustment, it does not diminish what you contributed or who you are.

Retirement, whether chosen or forced, planned or sudden, is not the end of your value. It is the end of one chapter and the beginning of another. And you are allowed to close the chapter before it closes itself.

If you are reading this and still wrestling with guilt, ask yourself this, if a friend came to you in the same situation, exhausted, unwell, struggling — would you tell them to keep going? Or would you tell them it was time to stop?

You deserve the same kindness you would offer them.

Leah did not leave that day with a final decision. But she did leave with something more useful — the recognition that what was happening was real, and that listening to it was not a sign of weakness.

Leaving is not failure. Sometimes, it is the bravest and most self-respecting choice a person can make.

Where This Leaves You

If you started this chapter wondering whether you were overreacting, I hope you now have a clearer answer. The exhaustion that weekends do not fix. The flatness where engagement used to be. The tears in the car park. These signs are not overreactions. They are information your body and mind have been sending for some time. They deserve to be taken seriously.

Recognizing that work may no longer be sustainable is not the same as admitting defeat. It is acknowledging reality. It is listening to signals you may have spent decades learning to override. And it is giving yourself permission to make a decision based on what is true now, not what you wish were true or what you think you should be able to handle.

This chapter has not asked you to force a final answer. It has asked you to pay attention to the signs your body, mind, and circumstances have been sending you, and to take them seriously. That matters, because before you can decide what to do next, you need a clearer sense of whether continuing work is still wise, safe, or sustainable. The next chapter will help you turn that clarity into a decision.

What to Take With You

The signs that work is no longer sustainable — persistent exhaustion, emotional flatness, physiological symptoms, and the car park cry — are not signs of weakness; they are data that deserve attention.

Burnout is not a character flaw or a lack of resilience; it is a response to chronic workplace stress that has not been successfully managed.

Choosing to retire because you are exhausted, unwell, or simply done is not failure — it can be wisdom, strategy, and an act of self-respect.

Questions Worth Asking

What signals has your body or mind been sending you about work that you have been dismissing or overriding, and what would it mean to take those signals seriously?

If a close friend came to you in your exact situation — same exhaustion, same health concerns, same workplace conditions — what advice would you give them, and why is it hard to offer yourself that same kindness?

Try This Before You Move On – The Signal Inventory

Set aside 15 minutes. Take a sheet of paper and divide the page into four sections. Label each section with one of the following domains: Body, Mind, Work, Home Life.

Under each domain, write down the signs you have noticed in the past three months. Keep it honest and true. Do not explain it away. Do not argue with it. Just list what has been happening.

Then, mark each item: O = occasional, R = recurring, C = constant

When you are finished, look at the page as a whole and ask yourself: Are the signs showing up in one domain, or across several? Which signs are recurring or constant? Does this look like a rough patch, or a pattern that needs to be taken seriously?

Circle the domain or domains that concern you most.

Then complete the final sentence below to name the pattern, especially the signals that keep recurring or have become constant.

I can no longer ignore:

Chapter 3

The Decision Framework — Leave, Linger or Lighten the Load

Dakota had made plenty of difficult decisions in her career, but this one had a special talent for turning her brain into porridge. She could handle budgets, staff dramas, and last-minute crises without blinking. But when it came to her own retirement, she kept circling the same three options: leave now, linger a bit longer, or find some kind of middle path, but without feeling any clearer about which one actually fit.

She had spent the better part of six months asking herself whether she should retire, and the question had become so familiar it had started to feel like background noise. What she had not yet done was turn that question into a decision. Because a decision required more than worry, more than spreadsheets opened at midnight, more than vague reassurances from friends who meant well but had never stood where she was standing.

What Dakota needed was a way to sort the facts from the fear. A method that could hold the weight of the question without collapsing into panic or wishful thinking. Something more steady than her gut, clearer than her mood on any given Tuesday, and more reliable than the voice in her head that kept changing its mind depending on whether she had slept well or sat through another pointless meeting.

This chapter introduces the decision framework at the center of the book — the Leave, Linger, or Lighten the Load model. These are three realistic ways to respond when work is no longer fitting your life in the way it once did. It is not a personality quiz. It is not a financial calculator. It is a practical way of working out which of three realistic pathways best matches your current situation across health, money, work conditions, and emotional readiness.

Instead of asking one giant question — *Should I retire?* — The framework breaks the decision into three more manageable pathways by helping you answer three questions:

- ***Should I retire now*** because continuing is no longer safe, sustainable, or worth the cost?
- ***Should I wait*** because the timing is not quite right, but could be with a bit more preparation?
- ***Should I build a transition bridge*** because full retirement feels too far but staying in my current position is not working either?

Each pathway is valid. Each one requires different actions. And each one becomes clearer when you stop trying to answer all three at once.

Why Most People Get Stuck

The retirement decision can feel enormous because it is usually framed as one big, irreversible leap. You are either working or you are not. You are either in or you are out. That binary framing makes the decision feel riskier than it needs to be, and it ignores the reality that many people need something in between.

People also get stuck because retirement is not only a practical decision. It is tangled up with money, health, identity, fear, timing, loyalty, guilt, and the uncomfortable question of who you will be when work no longer organizes your days. No wonder the mind keeps circling. It is trying to answer too many questions at once.

The framework in this chapter gives you three pathways instead of two. It also gives you permission to choose the pathway that fits your life right now, rather than the one you think you are supposed to choose. It helps you assess your situation across four key areas: health, finances, work conditions, and emotional readiness. It also helps you recognize which signs point toward each pathway, name the option that best matches where you are now, and identify a practical next step. That might mean submitting your notice, strengthening your financial buffer, or designing a staged exit plan.

You will also get clearer on what each pathway actually involves, what it protects you from, and what trade-offs it requires. No decision is perfect. Some decisions are simply good enough to move you forward.

What You Do Not Need to Decide Yet

This chapter will not ask you to map out the next thirty years. It will not require you to know exactly what retirement will look like, what your purpose will be, or how you will fill your days. Those questions come later, and they are easier to answer once you have made the first call.

Right now, you just need to know whether you are going to leave now, linger a bit longer at work, or lighten your workload by building a transition bridge to full retirement. Everything else can wait.

A Note on Uncertainty

If you finish this chapter and still feel some uncertainty, that is normal. The framework is not designed to eliminate doubt. It is designed to reduce it enough that you can make a decision without talking yourself into paralysis. Certainty is a luxury most people do not get. What you can have instead is clarity about what matters most, and confidence that you are weighing the right things.

Dakota sat down one evening with a notebook, wrote three headings across the page, and started filling in what was actually true. Not what she hoped. Not what she feared. Just what was true. And for the first time in months, the fog started to lift.

The Three Pathways: Leave, Linger, or Lighten the Load

The three pathways are possible responses to your current reality. Each one protects you from different risks and comes with different trade-offs. The key is matching the pathway to what matters most right now — not what you wish mattered, or what you think should matter, but what actually does. In plain English, here is what each one means:

- **Leave** means stepping away now because continuing is no longer wise, safe, or sustainable.
- **Linger** means staying a little longer because a bit more time would put you in a stronger position to retire.
- **Lighten the Load** means reducing the pressure through a staged transition plan — fewer hours, a different role, consulting, contract work, or another middle path —rather than trying to jump straight from full-time work to full retirement.

Pathway One: Leave

This is the clean exit. Full retirement now. You stop working, hand in your lanyard, and step fully into retirement. No phased transition. No part-time arrangement. Just done.

This pathway tends to fit when continuing work is actively costing you too much — physiologically, emotionally, financially, or relationally. It may be the right choice when your health is deteriorating, your workplace has become untenable, or the cost of staying now outweighs the uncertainty of leaving.

Leave makes sense when:

- Your health is at risk if you continue, and your doctor has said so clearly
- Burnout has progressed past tiredness into something that feels unsafe
- Your workplace has become genuinely toxic, and staying is doing measurable harm
- Waiting longer will not improve your situation in any meaningful way, and may make it worse
- You have enough financial runway to cover at least the early transition without panic

Leave does not require you to be thrilled about retirement. It does not require a detailed plan for what comes next. It requires you to recognize that continuing in your current role costs more than stopping does.

The trade-off — you lose the income, structure, and identity that work provided, all at once. The path requires enough financial viability and enough emotional tolerance for the uncertainty that follows. Full retirement can be the safest choice, but it is also the most abrupt. The landing needs to be managed carefully, or the relief can turn into freefall.

The appeal of this option is clarity. Once the decision is made, you can direct your energy into landing well rather than enduring longer than is wise. The risk is that the sudden absence of work can leave a lot of unstructured time to manage. That does not mean retirement is a mistake. It means the landing needs some shape.

Pathway Two: Linger

Linger means staying in your current role for a defined period while you prepare more thoroughly. This is the "not yet" option. This is not just "keep going indefinitely". It is a deliberate, strategic delay with clear goals and an end date.

You stay in work for a defined period – a strategic wait - because doing so gives you something important — time to reach a financial milestone, time to sort paperwork, time to prepare emotionally, or time to test whether retirement is really what you want.

Linger makes sense when:

- You are close to a financial milestone that will make retirement significantly easier (pension eligibility, mortgage payoff, redundancy package)
- Your health and energy can sustain a defined period of waiting without serious harm
- You need time to build a better financial buffer, sort out paperwork, or test-drive retirement through extended leave
- Retiring now would create financial stress that another period of income would materially reduce

- You have a specific exit date in mind, and sticking it out feels manageable with that target visible

The trade-off — you stay in a situation that may be draining you, and you risk waiting too long if conditions worsen. Linger only works if you set a firm deadline and stick to it. This option prioritizes long-term stability over immediate relief, which is why it needs boundaries. Without a clear deadline, Linger can quietly become another way of postponing the decision.

This can be the wisest option when your work is still tolerable, your health is holding, and waiting a little longer would make retirement significantly easier. It is a strategic delay, not a passive one.

The appeal of this option is that it buys you preparation time. The risk is that "not yet" can slide into "not yet again" if you do not put boundaries around it. Strategic waiting works best when it has a deadline, a purpose, and a very clear sense of what you are waiting for.

Pathway Three: Lighten the Load

This is the middle path. Think of it as a transition plan — a bridge to retirement. You do not leave work entirely, but you stop trying to carry on in the same way. You reduce your work intensity by cutting hours, changing roles, consulting, taking contract work, or building some other staged exit that gives you breathing room without cutting income, structure, and connection all at once.

Lighten the load makes sense when:

- Full retirement feels too abrupt, but your current workload is unsustainable
- You need ongoing income, but not at the cost of full-time stress
- You want to test what retirement might feel like without committing entirely
- Your workplace offers flexible arrangements, or you have skills that translate to freelance or casual work
- You are not ready to lose your work identity completely, but you need breathing

space

This option often fits when full-time work is no longer sustainable, but full retirement is not yet financially comfortable or emotionally appealing. It is also a good fit for people who need to step down without stepping off a cliff.

The appeal of a bridge plan is flexibility. It can protect health, preserve income, and soften the identity jolt that sometimes comes with a full stop.

The trade-off is that a bridge plan requires design. Bridge plans do not usually happen by accident. They need thought, negotiation, boundary-setting, and the discipline to stop part-time work from quietly creeping back into full-time hours. They require a realistic sense of what kind of work you can still do without recreating the problem you were trying to escape.

Bridge plans can also delay the full psychological shift into retirement, which may feel unsettling for some people. The benefit is that you keep some structure while you ease into the next stage. The risk is that you may stay partly attached to a work identity you are trying to loosen.

The Four Decision Areas That Matter Most:

Retirement decisions are rarely driven by one factor alone. Research on retirement adjustment points to several realities that shape how people manage the transition, including health, finances, exit conditions, social participation, and relationships.[2,4] Once you stop treating retirement as one giant yes-or-no question, the next step is to look at the four areas that tend to carry the most weight in the decision. For this chapter, we will translate that into four decision areas: **health, money, work conditions, and emotional readiness.**

Health

Can your body and mind sustain what you are doing now?

Not in theory. Not if you grit your teeth and keep going. In reality.

Health is not only about diagnoses. It is about sleep, energy, blood pressure, mood, concentration, recovery time, and whether work is making you less well than you were a year ago. If continuing is causing measurable harm, health moves from "important consideration" to "hard constraint."

Money

Can you afford to retire now, or would waiting materially improve your position?

This is where fear often gets loud, so the aim is not to answer every possible money question all at once. It is to establish whether you have enough to cover essentials, whether waiting would meaningfully improve the picture, and whether a bridge plan would reduce the pressure without prolonging the damage.

You are not trying to solve the rest of your life in one sitting. You are trying to work out what is financially realistic now.

Work Conditions

Is the job still workable, or has it become harmful, unstable, or simply no longer worth the cost?

This area asks you to look honestly at your current work reality. Is the problem the work itself, the environment, the workload, the manager, the commute, the culture, or the cumulative wear and tear of all of it together? Can the current job be sustained safely for a little longer, or are you already beyond that point?

Sometimes the answer is retirement. Sometimes the answer is "not this job...not like this."

Emotional Readiness

Can you tolerate the uncertainty of leaving, and do you have enough steadiness to begin rebuilding?

You do not need to feel thrilled. You do not need a five-year purpose statement. You do need some ability to tolerate ambiguity, some willingness to let your identity shift, and enough emotional room to build a new rhythm after work stops organizing your days.

This area matters because people sometimes stay too long out of fear of the unknown, while others leave abruptly without noticing how much emotional scaffolding work had been providing.

The question is not whether you feel perfectly ready. Hardly anyone does. The question is whether you are ready enough for the path you are considering.

Clarifying Where You Stand

Recognizing the signs is one thing. Deciding what they mean for your next step is another. Before you rush toward an answer, it helps to pause and look clearly at where you stand right now, not in theory, not on a better day, but in the reality in which you are actually living.

The grid below is not a scoring system. It is a simple way to sort what is true without getting lost in your own head. You do not need perfect scores or a blazing moment of certainty. You just need to see which pathway has the fewest deal-breakers and the strongest fit across health, money, work conditions, and emotional readiness. If your answers are mixed, do not worry. That simply means your situation is mixed too. It shows you where the pressure points are – and that is valuable information.

To use the grid: Read across each row and highlight the cell that best matches your current reality. Then step back and look for the pattern.

A Simple Grid to Clarify Where You Stand

Sort what is true. You do not need perfect scores — just notice which pathway has the fewest deal-breakers.

Domain	LEAVE Full Retirement	LINGER Strategic Wait	LIGHTEN THE LOAD Transition Bridge
Health	Harm now, or doctor says work is unsustainable.	Tired, but stable enough to wait a defined period.	Full-time work is too much, but you are not in immediate danger.
Money	Enough runway for essentials, and waiting will not help much.	A financial milestone is close: mortgage, package, pension, or buffer.	You need ongoing income, but not at the current load.
Work conditions	Workplace is toxic, unmanageable, or changed beyond your control.	Job is tolerable enough while you prepare.	Current role drains you, but different or reduced work could fit.
Emotional readiness	You can tolerate uncertainty long enough to rebuild structure.	You need time to test, sort, or picture what comes next.	Full retirement feels too abrupt, but you need breathing room now.

Tip: Highlight any cell that feels like a deal-breaker. The pathway with the fewest deal-breakers is often the best fit for now.

By now, one pathway may be standing out more clearly than the others. Even if it is not, you may at least be able to rule out one or two options. That is enough to begin thinking about your next step.

For Dakota, this was where the fog started to lift. She was not confused about everything. She had simply been trying to answer one giant question instead of three smaller, more honest ones.

Naming Your Next Step

Once you have assessed where you sit across those four areas, your next step becomes clearer. Not certain. Just clearer.

If three or four factors point toward **Leave**, your next step is preparing to leave — setting an exit date, checking your financial buffer, and building a 90-day landing plan.

If most factors point toward **Linger**, your next step is setting a firm deadline and identifying what needs to happen before that date — strengthening savings, sorting paperwork, or taking extended leave to test the decision.

If the factors are mixed, or if full retirement is not financially viable yet, your next step is designing a transition bridge to **Lighten the Load** — exploring part-time options, calculating what reduced income you actually need, or negotiating a phased exit with your employer.

You do not need to solve everything today. You just need to name the pathway you are walking toward and the first action in that pathway.

Dakota wrote her next step at the bottom of her notebook page — Book appointment with retirement fund. Check part-time options at work. Set the decision deadline for the end of the quarter. Dakota still did not have perfect certainty. But she had stopped circling. She had a next step she could name, and that was enough to move the decision out of her head and into the world.

Where This Leaves You

The retirement decision does not require perfection. It requires clarity about which pathway you are standing in front of, and what walking through it will actually involve. **Leave, Linger, Lighten the Load** — each pathway is valid, each one protects you from different risks, and each one becomes manageable once you stop trying to solve all three at once.

What matters most is matching the pathway to your reality right now. Not the reality you wish you had, or the one you think you should have, but the one that is actually true when you assess your health, your money, your work conditions, and your emotional readiness honestly.

If your health is at risk, if your workplace has become toxic, or if continuing costs more than stopping does, **Leave** may be the only safe choice. If you are close to a financial milestone that will make retirement significantly easier, and your body and mind can sustain the wait, **Linger** may be the wiser call.

If full retirement is not workable right now, but continuing exactly as you are no longer makes sense, a **Lighten the Load** transition plan can give you time, income, and breathing space. That is not indecision. It is design.

What you are choosing now is not the rest of your life. You are choosing your next step — and next steps can be adjusted.

What will keep you stuck is continuing to ask the same enormous question without breaking it into smaller, answerable parts. The loop only breaks when you stop asking *What should I do?* and start asking *What does each option actually require, and which one fits my situation right now?*

Dakota's notebook exercise was not magic. It did not eliminate doubt or deliver perfect certainty. What it did was give her a method for sorting the facts from the fear. It helped her see that she was not choosing between success and failure, or between courage and cowardice. She was choosing between three legitimate pathways, each with different trade-offs, and each one requiring different actions.

By the time she closed her notebook, she had named her next step. Not because the decision was suddenly easy. But because she finally had a framework strong enough to hold the question.

That is what this chapter offers you. Not certainty. Not a guarantee that you will never second-guess yourself. Just a steadier way to assess where you are, what each pathway requires, and which pathway makes the most sense to walk through next.

The chapters that follow will help you prepare for what comes after you choose. But first, you need to choose. And now, you have a method for doing that without turning your brain into porridge every Tuesday night.

Write your three headings. Fill in what is true. Name your next step. And then take it.

The decision will not make itself. But it also does not need to be perfect. It just needs to be clear enough, honest enough, and good enough to move you forward.

What to Take With You

The retirement decision becomes more manageable when you stop treating it as one giant yes-or-no question and assess three realistic pathways — **Leave, Linger or Lighten the Load**

The four decision areas that matter most are health, money, work conditions, and emotional readiness. Looking at them separately makes the choice clearer.

You do not need perfect certainty to move forward. You need enough clarity to name your next step and act on it.

Questions Worth Asking

Which of the three pathways currently feels like the closest fit for my reality — **Leave, Linger or Lighten the Load** — and what makes that option feel more true than the others?

Of the four decision areas — health, money, work conditions, and emotional readiness — which one is carrying the most weight in my decision right now, and why?

Try This Before you Move On – Your Personal Pathway Check

Take a sheet of paper and divide it into four equal sections, as shown below. Label the sections **Health, Money, Work Conditions,** and **Emotional Readiness**.

Step 1. Under each heading, write the specific facts that are true for you right now. Do not write what you hope. Do not write what you fear. Write what is actually true. These might include things like a doctor's warning, poor sleep, a mortgage nearly paid off, a toxic manager, a call for redundancy packages, fear about losing structure, the possibility of part-time work, the need for another six months of income.

Health	Money
Work Conditions	**Emotional Readiness**

Step 2. Then look back at the grid in this chapter. For each item on your list, ask yourself whether it points more strongly toward Leave, Linger, or Lighten the Load. Mark it accordingly with L, Li, or LL.

Step 3. When you are finished, step back and look at the pattern. Which pathway has the strongest overall case? Which one has the fewest deal-breakers? Which one fits your actual life better than the others right now?

Step 4. Circle that pathway. What is the next step that would move you toward that pathway? Write down one concrete next step beneath it.

The point is not to produce a perfect answer. It is to sort your own reality clearly enough that the next move becomes visible.

Chapter 4

When Retirement Happens to You — Forced Exits, Health Crashes and Other Plot Twists

Frank had imagined his retirement would involve a farewell lunch, some good-bye-and-good-luck speeches, a farewell gift, handshakes from colleagues, and at least a few months to get his head around it. Instead, he got a Tuesday afternoon meeting, a restructure announcement, and a severance package that needed a response by Friday.

This was not the careful transition he had pictured. It was an unplanned exit, and he had no idea what he was supposed to do first.

Retirement is supposed to be a choice. A decision you make when you are ready, on your terms, with enough time to plan, prepare, and walk out with your dignity intact. But for many people, retirement does not arrive as a choice at all. It arrives as a redundancy letter. An injury that changes what you can manage. A new caring responsibility. A family crisis that forces a sudden move. A doctor's appointment that changes everything. Or simply the slow, grinding realization that you cannot keep doing this, and the decision has already been made for you by your body, your workplace, or circumstances you did not see coming.

If that is where you are right now, this chapter is for you.

Involuntary retirement is not the version anyone imagines. There is no leisurely countdown where you tick off the final weeks with a sense of accomplishment. Instead, there is shock. There is scrambling. There is the strange, disorienting experience of having the ground disappear beneath your feet while everyone around you carries on as if nothing has changed.

And yet much retirement advice still seems to assume you had time to prepare. It assumes you saw it coming. It assumes you had the luxury of planning, organizing, and making a calm, rational decision about when to go. If you did not have that luxury, much of the standard advice feels irrelevant at best and insulting at worst.

So let us be clear. If retirement happened *to you* rather than *with you*, you are not behind. You are not doing badly at something you were never given the chance to plan for. You are simply dealing with a different kind of transition, and that transition needs a different kind of map.

This chapter will not pretend that involuntary retirement is easy, or that you should feel grateful for the "opportunity" to stop working earlier than planned. It will not tell you that everything happens for a reason, or that this is secretly a gift in disguise. What it will do is help you stabilize. It will help you work out what needs your attention right now, what can wait, and how to regain a sense of control when the decision is taken out of your hands.

Because here is the truth. Even when retirement is forced, you still have choices. Not about whether you leave, but about how you land. Not about whether you had time to prepare, but about what you do with the time you have now. Not about whether the transition is messy, but about whether you let the mess define the next chapter.

When the Exit Is Not Really a Choice

There are many ways people get pushed toward retirement before they feel ready. Sometimes it is dramatic: a redundancy, a diagnosis, a workplace event that changes everything in a single afternoon. Sometimes it is quieter: a body that stops tolerating the workload, a caring role that expands until there is no room left for paid work, or a workplace culture that becomes so draining that leaving starts to feel less like a choice and more like an act of self-preservation.

What these situations have in common is not just the practical disruption. It is the loss of timing. You do not get to choose the moment carefully. You do not get to line up your finances, finish your projects, or rehearse the emotional landing. You are dealing with the fact that the script changed without consulting you first.

For Frank, that was the part that unsettled him most. It was not only that he was leaving, but that he had not had time to prepare the ground beneath his feet

That loss of control matters. It is one reason an unplanned exit can feel so destabilizing, even when part of you knows that leaving was necessary. You are not just adjusting to retirement. You are adjusting to the fact that it arrived in a form you did not ask for.

The Emotional Reality of a Forced Exit

The first response to a forced exit may be shock, even if you saw it coming. Then comes a complicated mix of feelings that do not always make sense together. Relief that the uncertainty is over. Anger that the decision was made without you. Grief for the version of your working life you thought you still had. Fear about money, identity, and what happens next.

Shock is common. So is anger. Grief often turns up too, even when you wanted out. You may feel relieved and frightened, vindicated and rejected, free and completely unmoored. None of that is contradictory. It is transition.

Research on retirement adjustment suggests that the conditions under which people leave work matter. Exit conditions are one of the factors associated with how people adjust to retirement, and involuntary retirement has also been linked with depression risk in longitudinal research.[4, 15] That does not mean everyone who is pushed out will struggle in the same way. It means the way you leave can shape the way you land.

For Frank, naming the shock mattered. It did not make the redundancy less abrupt or the grief less real, but it did stop him from expecting himself to respond as though this had been a calm, carefully chosen transition. People often assume that if work had become unbearable, leaving will feel like pure relief. Sometimes it does — for about six minutes. Then other feelings tend to barge in.

Forced retirement can also bruise the ego in ways that are hard to explain. If the exit involved redundancy, ill health, ageism, or simply being unable to sustain the pace anymore, it can feel as though your competence has been publicly questioned — even when the facts tell a different story. You may know, intellectually, that this is about circumstance. Emotionally, it can still feel personal.

That is why the first task is not to judge your feelings, tidy them up, or transform them into a meaningful lesson by Thursday. The first task is simply to recognize what has happened and stop expecting yourself to respond as though this were a calm, planned transition.

The First Thirty Days — Stabilization, Not Reinvention

The first month after a forced exit is not the time to reinvent yourself, launch a side hustle, or discover your true purpose while alphabetizing the pantry. It is the time to stabilize.

That means focusing on the basics. Facts before fantasies. Safety before self-improvement. Information before major decisions. The first thirty days are about reducing panic, gathering what you need, and avoiding the kind of frightened decisions that feel urgent in the moment and regrettable later.

Think of it as a temporary holding pattern. Not a permanent state. Not a sign that you are falling apart. Just a practical response to the fact that, under stress, everything can feel more urgent, more confusing, and more impossible than it did before. In plain English, that means this is not the best moment to redesign your entire life before dinner.

The first thirty days are not about reinventing your life. They are about taking the first **STEP: Stabilize, Take stock, Establish a routine, and Pick one decision** that buys you time and steadier ground.

Week One: STABILIZE

In the first week, your job is not to work out the rest of your life. Your job is to steady the ground beneath your feet. Stop. Breathe. Do not decide anything major.

Tell someone what has happened. Write down the basic facts — your last day, any severance or leave entitlements, what income is still coming in, and what decisions have immediate deadlines attached to them. Check your immediate money situation — bills due, accessible funds, and any urgent matter that cannot be ignored. Then, as much as possible, rest and let your nervous system settle.

Shock can make ordinary things feel strangely difficult. Simple tasks feel larger than they should. Minor decisions take up more room than they deserve. If you are exhausted, frightened, or struggling to think clearly, that is not a character flaw. It is a human response to stress.

Week Two: TAKE STOCK

By the second week, you can start gathering information without demanding certainty from yourself.

Contact your retirement fund, pension provider, or super fund and ask about your options. Check your health insurance status and coverage. Review any severance package properly. Start tracking actual spending so you know what your current reality looks like, not what panic says it looks like.

This is the week for facts, not catastrophes. You are not trying to solve retirement in one grand sitting. You are trying to reduce the number of unknowns.

Week Three: ESTABLISH A TEMPORARY ROUTINE

By week three, you need structure. Not a perfect retirement schedule. Just something that stops the days from blurring into each other.

Set a wake-up time. It does not have to be early, but it should be consistent. Get dressed. Leave the house at least once a day, even if it is just to walk around the block. Plan one small thing each day that gives you a sense of purpose or accomplishment. It might be sorting a drawer, calling a friend, or cooking a proper meal. It does not matter what it is. It just needs to be something you can point to at the end of the day and say, "I did that."

This is not about productivity. This is about preventing drift. In the early weeks of an unplanned exit, it is very easy to let the days shrink around you. A small routine helps keep the world from getting too narrow.

Week Four: PICK ONE DECISION

By the end of thirty days, you may be stable enough to make one decision. Not all the decisions. Just one.

It might be: "*I am going to check whether I can access retirement savings, pension funds, superannuation, or other income support while I recover.*"

It might be: "*I am going to look for part-time work to bridge the gap until I can access my pension.*"

It might be: "*I am going to talk to a financial adviser because I cannot work this out on my own.*"

Whatever it is, it should be a decision that buys you time, not one that locks you into a path you are not ready for. The goal is not to solve retirement in thirty days. The goal is to stabilize enough that you can start thinking about what comes next without panic doing the thinking for you.

By the end of the month, Frank still did not have a full retirement plan. What he had was steadier ground — enough information, enough rest, and one decision that bought him time instead of panic.

Where This Leaves You

Involuntary retirement is not the version anyone plans for, but it is the version some people get. If that is where you are right now, the most important thing to understand is this — you are not behind. You are dealing with a different kind of transition, and it requires a different kind of response.

When retirement is forced — whether through redundancy, health crisis, workplace restructure, or the slow grind of circumstances you could not control — the first job is not to build the perfect new life. It is to stabilize. To get from shock to solid ground without making frightened decisions that cost you later. The thirty-day stabilization plan in this chapter is not about solving everything. It is about buying yourself time, clarity, and breathing room. It is about separating what needs your attention right now from what can wait. It is about regaining a sense of control when the decision was taken out of your hands.

You did not choose this timing. But you can still choose what happens next. You can choose to rest instead of panic. You can choose to gather information rather than catastrophize. You can choose to build a temporary routine that stops the days from blurring into each other. And you can choose to make one decision, just one, that moves you from survival mode toward something that feels more like a plan.

Involuntary retirement brings grief, and that grief is real. You are allowed to feel angry that the decision was not yours. You are allowed to feel scared about money, identity, and what comes next. You are allowed to feel relief and terror at the same time. None of those feelings mean you are doing this wrong.

But here is what I have seen, both in my own life and in the lives of colleagues who were pushed out before they were ready — an unplanned exit does not mean an unmanageable future. It means a messier start. It means more scrambling and less ceremony. It means closing gaps you did not have time to address before you left. But it does not mean you cannot land well. It just means the landing looks different. Some of the steadiest retirements I have witnessed began with redundancy letters, health scares, and meetings that changed everything.

The people I have seen navigate those transitions most steadily were not the ones who pretended it was fine. They were the ones who named the reality, stabilized what they could, and gave themselves permission to rebuild at a pace that matched their circumstances.

You are four chapters into this book, and by now you may have a clearer sense of whether retirement is a choice you are making or a reality you are managing. If it is the latter, this chapter has given you a map for the first thirty days. The next chapters will help you with what comes after — the money questions, the identity shifts, the relationship renegotiations, and the practical work of building a life that fits.

But for now, if you are still in shock, still scrambling, still trying to work out what just happened — your only job is to stabilize. One day. One decision. One step at a time.

You did not get the retirement you imagined. But you can still get one that works.

What to Take With You

Involuntary retirement — through redundancy, health crisis, or workplace pressure — is common, disorienting, and not a reflection of your competence or worth.

The first thirty days are about stabilization, not optimization. Your job is to gather information, reduce panic, and avoid frightened decisions you will regret later.

Even when retirement is forced, you still have choices — not about whether you leave, but about how you land and what you do with the time you have now.

Questions Worth Asking

What is the one thing causing you the most anxiety right now, and what is one small action you could take this week to reduce that anxiety?

If you had to describe your current emotional state in one sentence, what would it be — and who could you say that sentence to out loud?

Try This Before You Move On — The 30-Day Stability Checklist

Use this checklist to guide your first month. Tick off each item as you complete it, and remember — progress, not perfection.

Week One — STABILIZE

- Tell someone what has happened
- Write down the facts (last day, severance, entitlements)
- Check immediate money situation (bills due, accessible funds)
- Rest and let your nervous system settle

Week Two — TAKE STOCK

- Contact retirement or super fund and ask about options

- Check health insurance status and coverage
- Review severance package properly
- Start tracking actual spending

Week Three — ESTABLISH A TEMPORARY ROUTINE

- Set a consistent wake-up time
- Leave the house once a day
- Plan one small daily task
- Check in with doctor if sleep, appetite, or mood are still severely affected

Week Four — PICK ONE DECISION

- Choose one action that buys you time and stability
- Write it down and commit to it
- Acknowledge what you have managed in thirty days.

Chapter 5

How Not to Panic About Money — Know Your Numbers Without the Spiral

Michael had opened the retirement calculator four times in the past week, entered his numbers, stared at the result, and closed his laptop without saving anything. The problem was not that he lacked information. It was that every time he looked at it, his brain leapt straight from *Can I afford to retire?* to *I will be eighty-three, broke, and living on toast.* What he needed was not more numbers, but a simpler way to work out what actually mattered right now.

Money is often the loudest voice in the retirement conversation, and rarely the calmest. It is the thing that keeps people awake at three in the morning, the reason they open spreadsheets and close them again without saving, and the subject that can turn a perfectly reasonable person into someone Googling how long will my savings last if I live to ninety-seven while staring at the kettle as if it might have the answers. The problem is not usually that people lack information. It is that they have too much of it, none of it feels certain, and their brain has decided to fill the gaps with catastrophe.

This chapter will not teach you how to invest, build a portfolio, or optimize your pension or retirement savings for maximum growth. There are other books for that, written by people with better calculators and stronger feelings about compound interest. What this chapter will do is help you separate money panic from money reality. It will show you how to identify the few numbers that actually matter for deciding whether you can retire now, wait a bit longer, or build a transition plan. It will help you create a rough first-year money picture without drowning in spreadsheets, and it will show you how to spot the costs that catch people off guard when the regular pay stops.

The goal here is not perfection. It is clarity. You do not need to map out the next thirty-five years in precise detail. You need to know whether retirement looks financially possible right now, what gaps need attention, and what your first year might roughly cost.

Most people approaching retirement fall into one of three camps. The first group has done all the sums, checked every account, and built a color-coded spreadsheet that would make an accountant weep with joy. They are not reading this chapter. The second group knows roughly what they have, has a vague sense of what they spend, and is hoping it will all work out. The third group has been avoiding the whole subject because looking at the numbers feels too frightening, too boring, or too much like admitting that retirement is actually happening.

If you are in the second or third group, this chapter is for you.

You will learn how to check the numbers that matter without getting swept up into every possible worst-case scenario. You will learn how to track what you are actually spending now, estimate what retirement might cost, and work out whether the gap between the two is manageable or whether you need a different plan. You will also learn when it is time to stop Googling and talk to a professional — and how to prepare for that conversation so it is actually useful.

Money does not have to be the thing that decides everything. But it does need a seat at the table. And that conversation works better when it is based on reality, not panic.

Let us start with the numbers that actually matter.

The Numbers That Actually Matter (And the Ones That Just Feed the Spiral)

For Michael, this was the first useful shift. He stopped treating every possible future scenario as equally important and focused instead on the handful of numbers that actually mattered right now. That did not make the money question fun, but it did make it less shapeless.

When people say they need to "sort out the money," they often mean they need to look at everything — every account, every investment, every possible future scenario, every what-if between now and age ninety-seven. That approach does not create clarity. It creates paralysis.

The truth is, you do not need to know everything. You need to know enough to make a decision. And "enough" is smaller than you think.

Official retirement budgeting guidance recommends estimating both income and outgoings before deciding what retirement may cost.[16, 17] You are not building a fantasy budget for a retiree with excellent self-discipline and no dental problems. You are building a working number, based on how your life is likely to work, not how an imaginary retiree might live.

For the purposes of this chapter, there are **four numbers you need first** when deciding whether you can retire now (**Leave**), wait a bit longer (**Linger**), or build a transition plan (**Lighten the Load**). Everything else is either detail you can sort later, or noise that feeds the panic.

Number One: What You Actually Spend Now

Not what you think you spend. Not what you wish you spent. What you actually spend. If you can track three to six months, even better.

This is the number most people avoid because it feels tedious and slightly shameful. But it is also the number that anchors everything else. If you do not know what you spend now, you cannot estimate what retirement will cost. And if you cannot estimate what retirement will cost, every other calculation is just guesswork wrapped in anxiety.

You do not need a complex system. A simple spreadsheet, a notebook, or a banking app that categorizes transactions will do. The goal is not perfection. It is pattern recognition. Official retirement budgeting guidance commonly starts with understanding current spending and likely retirement costs.[16, 17] You are looking for the baseline — rent or mortgage, utilities, groceries, insurance, transport, medical costs, and the discretionary spending that quietly adds up.

Number Two: What Retirement Is Likely to Cost in the First Year

Once you know what you spend now, you can estimate what retirement might cost. Retirement spending is not always the same as working-life spending. Some costs drop. Others stay stubbornly the same. A few may rise when people least expect it. A better starting point is your actual current spending, *adjusted* for what is likely to change.

Some costs may fall, some may rise, and some will sit there stubbornly refusing to participate in your retirement fantasy. Commuting, professional clothing, and weekday convenience spending may fall. But groceries may rise if you are home more. Electricity can rise for the same reason. Health costs may increase. So can leisure spending, at least in the early months, because freedom has a way of encouraging lunches out, small trips, and purchases that feel entirely deserved.

Your first-year retirement estimate is not one number you simply find. It is a working number you build by adjusting your current spending for the costs likely to fall, stay the same, rise, or catch you off guard. This number includes ordinary living costs, expected changes, and a small buffer for irregular but foreseeable expenses. This is where the rough estimate starts to take shape. Once you know what you spend now, the next step is to sort those costs into four broad groups — what is likely to drop, what will probably stay much the same, what may rise, and what may surprise you. You are not aiming for forensic precision here. You are building a realistic first-year picture, one category at a time.

Costs that usually drop

Work-related expenses often disappear or shrink. Commuting costs, whether gasoline or public transport. Work clothes, dry cleaning, and the shoes you only wore to the office. Professional fees and memberships. Daily takeaway coffees bought out of exhaustion and inconvenience. The odd lunch purchased because there was no time to pack one. These do not always disappear entirely, but they often shrink. Childcare, if that still applied. Contributions to your pension, superannuation, or retirement fund may also change once you stop working.

For some people, these add up to hundreds of dollars a month. For others, it is less. Write down what you actually spend on work-related costs now and subtract it from your retirement estimate.

Costs that usually stay the same

Some costs do not change much in the first year of retirement. Not unless you move, downsize, or suddenly decide to live on a boat. Mortgage, if you still have one, or rent. Rates and utilities. Phone bills. Internet. Streaming subscriptions quietly nibbling away in the background because you keep forgetting to cancel. Insurance too — health, car, home, life.

These are the expenses people sometimes underestimate because they are so ordinary they fade into the background. They form the floor of your retirement budget.

Costs that often rise

Healthcare may increase, particularly if you were covered by workplace health insurance and now need to arrange your own. Prescriptions, dental work, glasses, physical therapy, and the appointments you have been putting off for years because you were too busy working can all change the picture.

Leisure and discretionary spending can also rise, especially in the first year when you finally have time to do things. Travel, hobbies, eating out more often, gifts, entertainment. Not because you are being reckless, but because you are no longer too tired to leave the house.

Home maintenance and repairs often get attention once you retire because now that you are home long enough to notice things, the house starts presenting you with a list.

Seeing the categories separately can stop the whole exercise from feeling like one giant, unhelpful lump. The goal is to build a rough first-year picture that reflects how you are actually likely to live. This is not a perfect number. It is a working number. And a working number is enough to move forward.

The Hidden Costs That Ambush the Budget

This is where retirement budgets can get caught out. It is rarely the big, obvious expenses that throw people off. It is the accumulation of smaller or irregular costs that arrive without fanfare and then insist on being paid anyway. They may not belong in the monthly budget, but they do belong somewhere in the plan. Car registration and insurance do not stop just because you are retired. Neither do rates, utilities, or the subscriptions you forgot you were paying for.

And then there are the quiet costs. The ones that do not ask for attention every month but can make a very convincing claim on your money when they arrive. These are the costs that can sit outside the neat monthly budget but still need a place in the retirement plan: healthcare, maintenance, family support, and inflation.

Healthcare is a major one. Retirement guidance notes that out-of-pocket health costs can still arise even when public programs, Medicare-style systems, or private insurance are in place.[18] That is not a reason to panic. It is a reason to put health costs in the estimate rather than leaving them in the fog.

Home maintenance is another. The hot water system does not become more considerate because you are retired. Neither does the roof, the car, the air-conditioner, or the tree that suddenly decides to lean at an expensive angle.

Family support can also become a drain that people do not budget for properly. Helping adult children, contributing to travel for family events, paying for grandchildren's gifts, stepping in when someone is struggling — individually, these may seem manageable. Collectively, they can take a bite out of cash flow.

Then there are the one-off costs that feel as though they should have been predictable but somehow were not. Funerals, estate administration, urgent travel, major car repairs, and replacing appliances can all arrive as irregular but very real expenses.

Inflation quietly raises the floor under everything. Even modest annual price increases can make a budget that felt manageable in year one feel tighter by year three, especially if you have not built in some room to move.

Once the spending side has a realistic shape, the next question is whether your reliable income can meet it.

Number Three: What Income You Can Reliably Count On

The keyword here is *count on*. Not might. Not possibly. Not if everything goes well.

This is the steady money — the income likely to arrive with some reliability, such as:

- pension income, if eligible
- regular income from retirement savings, if that is already part of the plan
- investment income
- rental income, if you have it
- part-time income or consulting work, if that is part of the plan

Add it up. Write it down. This is your floor.

When people get themselves into a panic about retirement, it is often because they lump guaranteed income together with speculative income and then act surprised when the totals look murky. Separate the solid from the hypothetical. The solid number is the one that matters first.

Number Four: What Accessible Savings or Reserves You Have

Number Three is about money coming in. Number Four is about money already there. This is not monthly income. It is money already sitting there — the cash, savings, accessible retirement funds, or other liquid or semi-liquid reserves that could support the transition or cover a shortfall if needed.

This is also where your emergency fund belongs. An emergency fund is not part of your ordinary retirement spending estimate. It is money set aside for costs you are not planning for at all — the urgent, the disruptive, and the deeply inconvenient. If you already have emergency savings, note how much is available and how quickly you could access it. If you do not, that does not mean retirement is impossible, but it does mean the plan has less shock absorption.

This is not about producing a dramatic total and then either congratulating yourself or feeling ill. It is about knowing what liquid or semi-liquid resources are actually available to support the transition.

What do you have in retirement savings? What cash savings are accessible? What money is earmarked for emergencies rather than everyday spending? What can be drawn on, and when? We are not talking about the value of your house unless you plan to sell it or draw on equity. Not your car. Not your furniture. The clearer you are about this, the easier it becomes to judge whether retirement is possible now, safer later, or better approached through a transition plan.

This is also the point at which many people discover they have been carrying around either too much fear or too much optimism. Facts help with both. If the gap between your reliable income and your estimated costs is small, and your reserves are reasonable, you might be fine. If the gap is large and your reserves are modest, you need a different plan.

There is one more question that matters, but it does not need to be solved before you can make a rough first-year decision — how long the money needs to last. That is a longer-range planning question. For now, the goal is simpler — to build a working first-year picture that is clear enough to help you judge whether leaving now looks realistic, waiting makes more sense, or a transition plan is the wiser path.

How to Build a Buffer Without Panicking

A buffer is not a luxury. It is the difference between a surprise and a crisis. As noted earlier, an emergency fund sits with your accessible savings or reserves. A buffer is different. The buffer belongs in your first-year retirement estimate because it covers irregular but foreseeable costs — the things that do not happen every month but are still part of ordinary life.

Emergency fund guidance recommends setting accessible money aside for costs you are not planning for at all, such as urgent travel for a family crisis, a major unexpected repair, or another event that forces immediate spending.[19] Think of the buffer as the money that makes the first-year budget more realistic. Think of the emergency fund as the money that helps the plan hold together when life goes completely off script.

For a rough first-year retirement estimate, consider adding a buffer of 10 to 20 percent of your annual expenses — enough to cover the irregular, the awkwardly timed, and the expensive-but-not-shocking without derailing the whole plan.

If your estimated annual retirement spending is $50,000, that means a buffer of $5,000 to $10,000 in a separate account. Not invested. Not locked away. Just sitting there, boring and available, for the hot water system, the dental work, and the car registration.

If a full buffer feels out of reach right now, start smaller. Even $2,000 set aside for "life happening" is better than nothing. You can top it up over time as your retirement spending settles and you get a clearer sense of what the irregular costs actually look like.

The buffer is not about predicting every possible expense. It is about giving yourself room to breathe when irregular but foreseeable costs show up. Because it will. Dental work, car registration, home maintenance, and replacing an aging appliance are not usually emergencies. They are life doing what life does, with poor timing and no manners.

Building a First-Year Money Picture Without Drowning in Spreadsheets

Once you know the four numbers that matter most, the next step is building a picture of what your first year might actually cost. Not a detailed, line-by-line budget that accounts for every coffee. Not a thirty-year projection that tries to predict inflation, market crashes, and whether you will still be buying birthday presents in 2047. Just a simple, realistic estimate of what the first twelve months might look like.

This is where most people either drown in spreadsheets or avoid the task entirely. Both responses are understandable. One feels overwhelming. The other feels terrifying. What you need is a middle path — enough detail to be useful, not so much that you never finish.

A simple way to build a rough first-year estimate is this — start with what you actually spend now over twelve months. If you tracked three to six months of expenses as suggested earlier, you already have the baseline. If you have not done that yet, do it now. You cannot estimate retirement costs without knowing what your current life actually costs to run.

Once you have that number, adjust it for retirement. Subtract the costs likely to fall, add the costs likely to rise, and add a buffer for hidden or irregular expenses. What you are left with is not a perfect budget. It is a working number — enough to help you judge whether retirement looks possible now (**Leave**), safer later (**Linger**), or more realistic with a transition plan (**Lighten the Load**).

Once you have that number, compare it with the income you can count on. If your reliable income covers it comfortably, leaving may be more realistic. If the gap is small but uncomfortable, lingering may make sense. If the numbers work only with some ongoing income, that may point you toward lightening the load rather than stopping completely.

A Practical Example: How One or Two Big Costs Can Change the Decision

Before doing the numbers for your own situation, it helps to see how this kind of rough estimate works in practice. Michael's example shows why the decision is not always about every tiny expense. Sometimes one or two large recurring costs can change the whole shape of the picture.

Scenario A — Current Situation

In his current situation, Michael spends about **$77,040** a year. After adjusting for retirement — subtracting about **$6,500** in work-related costs, adding about **$7,000** in costs likely to rise, and allowing a **$5,000** buffer for irregular expenses — his rough first-year retirement budget comes to **$82,540**.

His reliable income is about **$64,000**, leaving a gap of **$18,540**. On those numbers, Leave looks too tight. Michael's better fit is probably Linger or Lighten the Load. He does not need to panic, but he does need to test whether another year of income, reduced work, or a major cost reduction would change the picture and move him into a stronger position.

Scenario B — Key Changes

In this scenario, two major costs disappear. **Michael's** mortgage is paid off, and the school fees end. His regular annual spending falls to **$36,240**. With the same retirement adjustments, his revised first-year retirement budget becomes **$41,740**. His reliable income remains **$64,000**, leaving a surplus of **$22,260**.

Suddenly, Leave looks much more realistic. With the mortgage and education costs removed, Michael's numbers shift from strained to workable, so his next step would be to confirm the plan is sustainable and then prepare for the practical side of leaving well.

The lesson is not that everyone should pay off a mortgage before retiring. That decision depends on **careful checking of** interest rates, tax, access to funds, cash reserves, pension or superannuation rules, and personal circumstances; preferably with qualified advice. It is included here only to show how removing a major recurring cost can change the shape of the decision.

The lesson is that large recurring costs can carry more weight than dozens of tiny ones. A rough money snapshot helps you see which costs are shaping the decision, which pathway fits now, and what would need to change before another pathway becomes possible.

When It Is Time to Talk to a Professional

There is no prize for doing all of this alone. Sometimes the breakthrough is not a spreadsheet epiphany at the kitchen table. It is one good conversation with someone who can help you see the numbers clearly.

If your money picture is straightforward, this chapter may be enough to help you make a first-pass decision. But if you are dealing with multiple income sources, tax complications, early access questions, a redundancy package, or a significant gap between income and likely costs, it is sensible to get professional advice.[20] Sometimes you are not as far from **Leave** as you think — but you may need to change one or two big things first.

The best reason to talk to a professional is not that you are incapable. It is that you do not need to spend six sleepless weeks trying to reinvent a job someone else already does.

Go into that conversation prepared. Bring your current spending, your estimated retirement costs, your income sources, your savings position, and your questions. Do not arrive with a vague sense of dread and hope the adviser can read your aura. The clearer your inputs, the more useful the advice will be.

Where This Leaves You

Money does not have to be the thing that decides everything. But it does need a seat at the table, and that seat works better when it is occupied by facts instead of fear.

By now, you should have a clearer sense of the four numbers you need first — what you spend now, what retirement might cost in the first year, what reliable income you can count on, and what accessible savings or reserves you have. You should also have a rough first-year picture that accounts for the costs that may drop, the ones that stay much the same, the ones that may rise, and the irregular expenses that need a buffer rather than a panic response. None of this makes you a financial expert. It makes you informed enough to decide whether retirement looks possible now, whether you need to wait, or whether a transition plan buys you the time and income you need to land more safely.

Michael did not emerge from the process suddenly loving spreadsheets. But he did come away with something far more helpful — a clearer sense of what was true, what needed attention, and what no longer needed to be dramatized at midnight.

If the gap between your income and your costs is small, and your reserves are reasonable, you may be fine. If the gap is large, or your buffer is thin, you still have options. You can adjust your spending. You can delay retirement by a year or two. You can build a transition plan that brings in part-time income while you shift. You can talk to a financial adviser or another qualified professional (not your cousin's sister's boyfriend, unless he *is* a financial advisor) who can help you close the gaps you cannot close on your own.

What you cannot do — what does not help anyone — is make the decision in a panic. Money fear is loud, persuasive, and often much less accurate than a boring list of actual numbers.

You do not need to know everything. You do need to know enough.

And enough, in this case, is wonderfully unglamorous — what comes in, what goes out, what might change, and how much room you have when life behaves like life. That is not a thrilling financial philosophy. But it is usually enough to make a sound decision.

What to Take With You

You do not need to know every possible future financial scenario. You need to know the few numbers that actually matter for the decision in front of you.

The most useful retirement money check is practical, not heroic — current spending, likely retirement costs, reliable income, available savings, and a buffer for surprises.

Money panic and money reality are not the same thing. Facts may still be confronting, but they are far easier to work with than dread.

Questions Worth Asking

Which part of the money question have I been avoiding most — tracking spending, estimating retirement costs, checking savings, or asking for help — and why?

If I looked only at the four numbers that matter, rather than every possible worst-case scenario, what would become clearer?

Try This Before You Move On — The Rough Money Reality Snapshot

Set aside 30 minutes and create a simple one-page money snapshot using the prompts below as a guide.

Step 1. Add up what you actually spend now over 12 months.

Step 2. Subtract the costs likely to drop in retirement.

Step 3. Add the costs likely to rise.

Step 4. Add a buffer for hidden or irregular expenses.

Step 5. This gives your rough first-year retirement budget.

Step 6. Write down the reliable income you can count on.

Step 7. Subtract your rough first-year retirement budget from your reliable income.

Step 8. This shows you the gap or surplus.

Step 9. Write down what accessible savings or reserves you have available if the numbers are still tight.

Step 10. Look at the big picture. What does it suggest?

- If your reliable income clearly covers your rough first-year retirement budget, **Leave** may be realistic.
- If the gap between your reliable income and your rough first-year retirement budget is small but uncomfortable, **Linger** may make more sense.
- If your rough first-year retirement budget can only be covered with some ongoing work income, **Lighten the Load** may be the better fit.
- If there is a gap, but your accessible savings or reserves could reasonably cover it for a time, you decide whether **Leave** may still be workable or another pathway would feel safer.

NOW, circle the biggest pressure point. Do not fix everything. Just identify the part that needs attention first.

Chapter 6

What Am I Retiring To? Identity, Purpose, and the Blank Page

Helena had been a senior engineer for 32 years, and on her first Monday of retirement she woke at 6:30 a.m. out of habit, made coffee, and sat at the kitchen table with absolutely no idea what to do next. The blank day stretched ahead of her like an accusation, and the thought that arrived, uninvited and unwelcome, was not excitement or relief, but a quiet, creeping panic: *Who am I now?*

Retirement, it turns out, is not just about leaving work. It is also about arriving somewhere else. And for many people, that somewhere else feels less like a destination and more like a blank page with no instructions.

When work falls away, it takes more than just the job with it. It takes structure. Status. A ready answer to the question *"So, what do you do?"* It takes the rhythm of your week, the shape of your day, and the quiet sense of being someone who matters in a specific, measurable way. What it leaves behind is space. And space, while theoretically appealing, can feel surprisingly uncomfortable when you are standing in the middle of it with no map.

This chapter is about what happens when the job title disappears and you are left with the question: *Who am I now?*

It is not a question most people expect to ask. Retirement is supposed to be about freedom, relaxation, and finally having time for yourself. And it is all those things, but it is also an identity shift. A renegotiation of self. A slow, sometimes awkward process of untangling who you were at work from who you are as a person.

For some, this transition feels natural. For others, it feels like grief. And for many, it feels like both at once.

The flatness, the uncertainty, the low-grade panic that can arrive on a Tuesday morning when you realize you have nowhere to be and no clear sense of what you are supposed to be doing — all of that can be part of the adjustment. It does not mean you have made a mistake. It means something significant has changed, and you may need time to find your footing.

This chapter will help you make sense of that adjustment. It will explore why identity shifts when work stops, why purpose does not arrive fully formed on day one, and how to move from the escape-fantasy version of retirement to one that actually fits your life. It will also help you avoid some of the traps people can fall into when trying to rebuild meaning too quickly or in ways that do not match their energy, values, or actual interests.

You will not be asked to reinvent yourself by Thursday. You will not be handed a list of hobbies and told to get busy. You will not be lectured about finding your passion or living your best life.

What you will get is permission to sit with the discomfort for a while. To acknowledge that losing a work identity is a real loss, even if the work itself was exhausting. To recognize that rebuilding a sense of self takes more than a weekend, and that the blank page in front of you is not a problem to solve — it is a space you get to fill slowly, carefully, and on your own terms.

Most importantly, this chapter works from one simple idea: identity after work is not something you find. It is something you build. One small, steady step at a time. And the first part of that process is understanding just how much of your old identity was tied to the work itself.

From *"What I Do"* to *"Who I Am"*: Untangling Identity from Job Title

For most of your working life, the question *"What do you do?"* has had a simple answer. You are a teacher. A manager. An engineer. A nurse. The job title does the heavy lifting. It tells people who you are, what you are good at, and where you fit in the world. It is shorthand for competence, status, and purpose. It is also, whether you meant it to be or not, a significant part of your identity.

Then you retire. And suddenly, the question does not have an easy answer anymore.

This is not a small adjustment. Research on retirement transition suggests that people do not all adjust in the same way, and that work-based role identities can shape how retirees experience the move out of paid work.[21, 22] The loss is not just about the work itself. It is about the loss of a clear, socially recognized identity that has been reinforced daily for decades.

At work, you knew who you were. You had a role. A desk. A title on your email signature. People needed you for specific things. You had expertise. You had status, even if you were tired of it. You had a reason to get up in the morning that did not require explanation or justification.

Retirement removes all of that. And what it leaves behind is not always clarity. Sometimes it is just... space. And the question: *who am I now?*

Why Job Titles Stick

The fusion between identity and occupation is not accidental. It is built over years of repetition, reward, and social reinforcement. Every time you introduce yourself at a meeting, sign an email, or explain what you do at a dinner party, you are reinforcing the link between your job and your sense of self.

Psychologists use the term "role identity" to describe the part of your self-concept that is tied to the roles you occupy.[23] For many people, work has been one of the dominant roles. It takes up time, generates external validation, and can provide a clear sense of contribution. When that role disappears, the identity attached to it does not simply transfer to something else. It has to be rebuilt. Slowly. And often awkwardly.

This is one reason some people feel flat or lost in the early weeks of retirement, even when they were desperate to leave. The relief of stopping is real. But so is the disorientation of no longer being the person you were at work. Once that work-based identity falls away, what some people notice first is not freedom, but the strange discomfort of all that empty space.

The Blank Page Problem

For Helena, the unsettling part was not only the empty Monday. It was the fear that she ought to know immediately what belonged in the space work had left behind. Once she stopped treating the blank page as a test, it became easier to notice what actually drew her.

One of the more unsettling aspects of retirement is the sudden absence of external structure. At work, your identity was partly defined by what other people needed from you. Meetings. Deadlines. Projects. Problems to solve. Retirement removes that external scaffolding, and you are left to define yourself from the inside out.

For some people, this feels liberating. For others, it feels like standing in front of a blank page with no idea what to write.

The instinct, often, is to fill the page quickly. To replace the work identity with something equally clear and impressive. Volunteer coordinator. Hobby expert. World traveler.

But rushing to fill the page can create a new problem. It can turn retirement into another performance — another attempt to produce a version of yourself that looks coherent from the outside, even if it does not fit from the inside. The pressure to have a meaningful plan immediately can be just as exhausting as the job you left.

A blank page is uncomfortable, but it is not a crisis. It is space before shape. And shape usually comes more slowly than people expect. That is one reason purpose can feel so elusive at first. People often expect it to arrive quickly, when in reality it usually takes time to emerge.

Why Purpose Takes Time

One of the more unhelpful retirement myths is that purpose should arrive in a blaze of clarity the moment work ends. As though, once you stop answering emails, your true calling will descend politely through the ceiling and introduce itself.

That is not usually how it works.

Purpose after work tends to emerge gradually. It often starts less as a grand mission and more as a handful of small clues — what draws your attention, what gives you energy, what kind of day feels satisfying, what kind leaves you flat. It is less lightning bolt, more slow pattern recognition.

This is one reason people can feel uneasy in the early months. They assume they should know what they are "retiring to," when in reality that answer may need to be built through trial, adjustment, and noticing what fits.

The first task is not to force meaning into place. It is to make room for it to appear.

In the absence of that emerging sense of purpose, many people fall back on a simpler version of retirement — the fantasy of escape.

The Escape Fantasy

Before retirement, people often imagine a version of life defined mainly by what disappears. No meetings. No alarm clock. No commute. No performance reviews. No Sunday dread.

That fantasy makes sense. When work has been exhausting, escape is part of the appeal.

But escape is not the same as identity. And relief, while real, is not the same as purpose.

Research on retirement adjustment suggests that people do not follow one single adjustment pattern, and that factors such as health, relationships, social participation, and meaningful activity can shape how the transition unfolds.[1,4] The difference is not about having a perfect plan. It is about having something concrete to move toward, rather than just something to escape from.

The problem with an escape-only version of retirement is that it gives you something to leave, but not much to move toward. That may be enough for the first few weeks. Eventually, though, relief needs somewhere to land.

The fantasy also tends to overestimate how much pure leisure you will actually want. Lying on a beach sounds appealing after a 60-hour work week. It sounds less appealing on day 43 of retirement when you have read all the books you meant to read and are starting to feel oddly restless.

The problem is not that the fantasy is false. It is that it is only half the picture. Again, sooner or later, relief has to be followed by something more solid.

From Fantasy to Fit

The shift from escape fantasy to real life requires asking a different kind of question. Not *"What do I want to stop doing?"* but *"What do I actually want my days to look like?"*

This is harder to answer than it sounds. Because the honest answer is often *"I do not know yet."* And that is fine. You do not need to know yet. But you do need to start paying attention.

Start by noticing what you already gravitate toward when you have unstructured time. Not what you think you should enjoy. What you actually enjoy. Do you like being around people, or do you need long stretches of quiet? Do you like projects with clear outcomes, or do you prefer open-ended exploration? Do you feel better when you are moving, or when you are still?

These are not trivial questions. They are the raw material of a retirement that fits.

You might also try testing small pieces of your retirement fantasy while you are still working. Take a week off and live it the way you imagine retirement might be. Sleep in. Go for walks. Spend a day doing nothing. See how it actually feels, rather than how you think it will feel.

Some people discover that their fantasy holds up. Others realize they need more structure, more purpose, or more social contact than they anticipated. Both discoveries are useful.

Once you begin to notice what fits, the next task is to build more of your life around it.

Building Toward Something

A more grounded retirement is usually built on more than escape. It needs addition too. Not only "finally free from work," but "finally able to focus on this thing that matters to me."

That thing does not need to be grand. It does not need to impress anyone. It just needs to be yours. And it needs to be specific enough that you can picture it, plan for it, and move toward it without waiting for inspiration to strike.

It might be caring for your health properly for the first time in years. It might be volunteering one morning a week. It might be learning something new, rebuilding friendships, writing, making, growing, mentoring, walking, or simply structuring your days in a way that no longer leaves you wrung out by 4 p.m.

The point is not to become a more impressive retiree. The point is to create a life that fits the person underneath the job title.

Helena still did not have a polished answer to *"What do you do now?"* But she had started to build a life that made that question feel less urgent. For now, that was enough.

Retirement is not a destination you arrive at fully formed. It is something you build, one small decision at a time, until it starts to feel like a life that fits.

Where This Leaves You

Retirement is not just about leaving work. It is about arriving somewhere else. And for many people, that somewhere else feels less like a destination and more like a blank page with no instructions, no job title to lean on, and no clear sense of who you are supposed to be now.

This is normal. It is also uncomfortable. And it does not mean you have made a mistake.

When work falls away, it can take more than just the job with it. It can take structure, status, and a ready-made identity that has been reinforced daily for decades. What it leaves behind is space. And space, while theoretically appealing, can feel surprisingly unsettling when you are standing in the middle of it with no map and no immediate sense of purpose.

The identity shift that can come with retirement is real, and it takes time. You do not need to have it all figured out in week one. You do not need a dazzling new purpose, a compelling answer to *"What do you do now?"*, or a beautifully curated retirement identity by next Tuesday.

What you need is enough patience to let the next version of your life take shape.

This chapter has tried to show that the discomfort is part of the adjustment. Something significant has changed. The old structure is gone. The old role has ended. The question now is not how quickly you can replace it, but what you want to build in its place.

That is why the move from escape fantasy to real fit matters so much. If retirement is built only on what you are relieved to leave behind, it can start to feel thin once the relief settles. But if it is built around things that genuinely matter to you — connection, contribution, curiosity, health, creativity, quiet, learning, or simply a better rhythm of life — it starts to feel more like an identity and less like an absence.

You do not have to find your whole future in one grand revelation. You can build it a piece at a time. A better Tuesday. A more fitting routine. A project that feels like yours. A life that no longer depends on a job title to make sense.

That is enough to begin.

What to Take With You

Retirement often involves an identity shift as much as a lifestyle shift. Losing the job title can feel disorienting, even when leaving work was the right decision.

Purpose rarely arrives fully formed on day one. It usually emerges slowly, through trial, attention, and noticing what genuinely fits.

The most sustainable retirements are shaped by what you are moving toward, not only by what you are leaving behind.

Questions Worth Asking

When I imagine retirement, what am I mostly imagining leaving behind — and what am I genuinely moving toward?

Outside my work identity, what kinds of activities, rhythms, or roles already feel most like me?

Try This Before You Move On – Who Am I?

Write the sentence: "Without my job title, I am someone who..."

Now complete it ten times.

Do not use your profession, former position, or anything linked to your status at work. Focus instead on qualities, values, interests, habits, and ways of being. Then underline the three responses that feel most true and the one that surprises you most.

That is not your finished retirement identity. But it is a very good place to start.

Chapter 7

Relationships, Routines, and Renegotiations — How Retirement Changes the House Rules

Noah had been retired for exactly eleven days when his partner looked up from her laptop during a work-from-home morning and said, with careful politeness, "I love you, but you need to stop reorganizing the kitchen while I am on video calls." He had not realized he was being disruptive — he had just been trying to be useful. What he had not yet understood was that retirement had not only changed his schedule; it was quietly reshaping the rhythm of the household and the unspoken rules that had governed it for years.

This chapter is about what happens when retirement moves in, starts rearranging the furniture, and develops surprisingly strong views about how the dishwasher should be loaded.

It is about the partner who suddenly has opinions about how the house should run. The retiree who cannot understand why their still-working spouse seems irritated by cheerful questions asked mid-meeting. The couple who love each other deeply but discover they have different ideas about how much togetherness is ideal, how quiet the house should be during the day, and whether lunch is a meal that requires consultation.

The good news is that these tensions, if they arise, do not mean the relationship is in trouble. They usually mean the old house rules may need updating. Once you can name what is changing, it becomes much easier to talk about it before resentment starts writing the script.

This chapter will help you think ahead about the relationship shifts retirement might bring. You will learn how to spot possible pressure points, have the awkward-but-necessary conversations early, and protect your relationship without giving up your need for space, autonomy, and a life that feels like yours.

Let us start with what might change, why it matters, and how to talk about it without turning everyday household irritation into a full domestic incident.

Same House, Different Time Zones: When Separate Routines Suddenly Collide

When one person retires and the other does not, the house suddenly contains two people living in fundamentally different realities. One person is operating on work time — alarms, deadlines, meetings, the need for quiet focus, and a rhythm dictated by external demands. The other is operating on retirement time — flexible mornings, no fixed schedule, and a day that can be shaped however they like. Retirement adjustment is not only individual; partners and household routines can become part of the adjustment process too. Their lives may now be in direct competition, and nobody warned them this would happen.[24, 25] In theory, this should be manageable. In practice, it can feel like trying to coordinate a dinner party across three time zones.

The still-working partner needs the house to function like a workplace during certain hours. They need predictability, minimal disruption, and the ability to concentrate without someone vacuuming outside the office door or asking cheerful questions about lunch plans. The retired partner, meanwhile, is trying to build a new life in the same space, and that life involves movement, activity, and the freedom to do things when the mood strikes. No one has done anything unreasonable. The problem is that two perfectly legitimate needs have started pulling against each other, often before either person has realised the rules have been quietly changing.

This collision shows up in small, surprisingly sharp ways. The retiree starts a load of laundry at 9:50 a.m., right before their partner is due online for a 10:00 meeting. The still-working partner snaps at the retiree for "hovering" when they were just walking through the room to get a glass of water. The retiree feels like a guest in their own home, tiptoeing around someone else's schedule. The working partner feels like their workspace has been invaded by someone who does not understand that work-from-home still means work.

One woman I spoke with during my own transition described it perfectly:

> "I retired in March. My husband kept working from home three days a week. By April, we had argued more about the television, the temperature in the house, and whether I was allowed to use the blender before noon than we had in the previous five years combined. It was not about the blender. It was about whose house this was now, and whose routine got priority."

She was right. It was not about the blender.

Different Setups, Different Pressure Points

The work-from-home version is only one version of this adjustment.

Sometimes one partner retires while the other still leaves the house for work every day. In that arrangement, the friction is less about noise during video calls and more about difference in tempo. One person is still living by alarms, deadlines, packed lunches, and the clock. The other is suddenly home with open hours and a day that feels far less structured. The still-working partner may come home tired and a little resentful that the retiree got to move more slowly. The retiree may feel awkwardly visible for doing exactly that.

Sometimes the tension is not interruption, but contrast. One person is still getting dressed for work, watching the clock, and heading out the door. The other is moving more slowly, sleeping later, or trying to work out what the day even is. Even in a loving relationship, that difference in rhythm can stir up envy, guilt, or low-grade resentment. Sometimes the working partner is not annoyed that the retiree is home. They are annoyed that they are not.

Sometimes one partner retires after the other has already retired. Then the issue is not competing time zones but constant overlap. The routines that once worked because each person had their own day now have to carry two people, full-time. Meals, chores, quiet time, television, outings, hobbies, and use of shared space all become more visible. The question stops being "Whose routine gets priority during work hours?" and becomes "How much togetherness actually feels good, and how much makes us want to fake an errand?"

In all of these arrangements, the house can quickly become a workplace, a recovery zone, a domestic space, and a proving ground for unspoken assumptions all at once.

The point is that there is no single retirement household model. Research on spousal retirement suggests that one partner's retirement can spill over into the other partner's daily life, wellbeing, and household arrangements.[24, 26] But what that looks like at home depends on the actual shape of the household — who is home, who is still working, who has already retired, and what expectations were quietly holding the old arrangement together.

Why the Little Things Get Loaded

Part of the problem is that these conflicts feel trivial, which makes them difficult to name without sounding petty. Nobody wants to be the person who starts a serious conversation about the rubbish bin, the untidy bench, or why one person now seems to have very strong views about when the washing should be done. But these small frictions accumulate.

They also carry more meaning than they first appear to. The issue is rarely just the task itself. It is not really about the bin, the bench, or who made lunch. It is about whose rhythm now sets the tone of the day, whose habits get to stay in place, and what each person assumes retirement is supposed to look like. One person may be trying to protect work time, another may be trying to protect quiet, another may be trying to protect autonomy, and another may simply be trying to work out what a useful day looks like now.

That is what makes this harder than it first appears. The practical irritations are real, but they are often standing in for bigger questions about space, fairness, usefulness, and how life is meant to run now that the old structure has gone. If those bigger questions stay unspoken, the small annoyances start doing too much emotional work.

From Assumption to Agreement

For Noah, the breakthrough was not the kitchen. It was the conversation. Once he and his partner stopped treating each irritation as a one-off annoyance and started talking about how the house was working now, the tension became easier to name and much less personal.

What helps is not pretending the adjustment should be easy. What helps is naming which version of the problem you are actually living.

Is one person still working while the other is trying to build a new routine? Are both people retired and now discovering they need more separateness than they expected? Is one person feeling guilty for not doing enough around the house, even though the other person is not asking for more? Are you dealing with practical friction, emotional pressure, or both?

Once you know which kind of tension you are dealing with, the conversation becomes easier and more useful. Not "You are driving me mad," but "I think we need to talk about how the house is working now, because the old routine no longer fits." Not "Everything is irritating," but "We need some clearer expectations about time, space, chores, and what each of us needs from the day."

What also helps is moving from assumption to agreement. That might mean agreeing on quiet times, shared times, separate times, who handles which household tasks, how much flexibility feels fair, and what no longer needs to be done the old way simply because that is how it used to be done. The goal is not perfect alignment. It is a household rhythm that feels livable for the people actually in it now.

Love, Space, and Not Losing Your Mind: Renegotiating Closeness Without Smothering Each Other

Retirement does not just change how much time you spend together. It changes the emotional texture of that time. When you have spent years passing each other in hallways, coordinating schedules via text, and catching up over dinner about days spent largely apart, the shift to constant proximity can feel less like togetherness and more like surveillance. Or suffocation. Or a low-grade awareness that someone is always there, which is lovely in theory and occasionally maddening in practice.

One of the most common — and least discussed — challenges of retirement is learning how to be close without being constantly together. How to share a home, a life, and a future without losing the autonomy, breathing room, and separateness that healthy relationships require.

This is not about whether you love your partner. It is about whether you can survive being in the same house, all day, every day, without one of you developing a sudden and inexplicable need to reorganize the garage for the third time this month.

Why More Time Together Is Not Always Better

Before retirement, most couples had built-in separateness. Work provided physical distance, mental space, and a rhythm that meant you were not constantly negotiating your day around someone else's presence. You had your world. They had theirs. You came back together in the evenings and on weekends, and that balance worked.

Retirement removes that structure. Suddenly, you are both home. All the time. And the habits, quirks, and routines that were invisible when you only overlapped for a few hours a day become impossible to ignore when you are sharing the same space from breakfast until bedtime.

Retirement may begin with one person's last day at work, but it soon finds its way into the shared spaces of the household. Research on couples adjustment to retirement suggests that partners affect each other's experience, especially when routines, expectations, and emotional rhythms have to be renegotiated.[24, 25, 27] That is why the decision to retire needs to be discussed as a household decision, not treated as one person's private project.

The problem is not that couples spend more time together. The problem is that they have not agreed on what that time should look like, how much of it should be shared, and how much separateness is still allowed.

One woman I know described it this way:

> "We had been married for 34 years. We loved each other. We liked each other. But three months into his retirement, I found myself hiding in the bathroom just to get ten minutes alone. Not because he was doing anything wrong. Just because he was always there."

She was not being dramatic. She was being honest. And her experience is far more common than most people admit.

Why This Conversation Feels Risky

Part of the difficulty is that wanting space from your partner can feel like a betrayal. You are supposed to want to spend time together. You are supposed to enjoy each other's company. Retirement is meant to be the reward for decades of hard work — finally, you get to be together without the distractions of jobs and deadlines.

Except for many people, constant togetherness does not feel like a reward. It feels like a loss of self. And admitting that out loud — to your partner, to yourself — can feel like admitting that something is wrong with the relationship, when in fact what is wrong is the assumption that more time together is always better.

The other problem is that couples often have wildly different expectations about how much closeness is ideal. One person imagines retirement as a return to companionship — shared meals, joint projects, long conversations, doing things together. The other person imagines it as freedom — finally having time to pursue their own interests, set their own schedule, and not have to coordinate every decision with someone else.

Neither vision is wrong. But if they are not compatible, and if they have not been discussed, retirement becomes a slow-motion collision between two people who thought they wanted the same thing but did not.

How to Protect Closeness and Autonomy

The first step is giving yourself permission to want space. Needing time apart does not mean your relationship is in trouble. It may simply mean that you are a person with your own rhythms, interests, and need for breathing room. Retirement does not remove that need. It just makes it harder to protect without deliberate effort. Most couples need both connection and breathing room. Retirement does not change that. It just makes the balance harder to protect without deliberate effort.

The second step is talking about it before resentment starts doing the talking for you. Not in the middle of an argument about whether someone is hovering, but in a calm moment, with curiosity rather than blame. The opening does not need to be perfect. It just needs to be honest enough to start the conversation:

> "I have been thinking about how we want to structure our days now that we are both home. I love spending time with you, and I also think I need some time to myself each day. Can we talk about what that might look like?"

The third step is creating practical boundaries that protect both shared time and separate time. This might mean agreeing that mornings are solo time. Or that certain rooms are personal space during certain hours. Or that each person gets to plan their own day without needing to check in constantly.

It might also mean scheduling time together, which sounds unromantic but is often necessary. If you do not actively plan shared activities, you can end up spending all day in the same house without actually connecting. Or worse, you spend all day in close proximity while each silently wonders why the other is suddenly always in the kitchen.

This is not about creating a rigid timetable. It is about making space for both people to land well.

Usefulness, Guilt, and the Myth of the Perfect Retired Household

Retirement has a nasty habit of exposing private standards people did not even realize they were carrying.

For some, it is the belief that a good retiree should be cheerful, organized, active, grateful, and finally on top of the spare room. For others, it is the belief that being home must now look like visible output — cleaner house, better meals, tidier cupboards, more evidence that the day amounted to something. And for others again, it is the sudden conviction that now they should be fixing, mowing, sorting, painting, repairing, or finally getting to every project the house has been quietly storing up for years.

The underlying pressure is the same, even if the tasks differ. The retiree feels they should now be visibly useful. The only thing that changes is the form that usefulness takes.

This can become especially tricky when the household itself is not demanding any of it. The retiree feels guilty. The partner feels fine. The retiree keeps apologizing for not having "done enough." The partner keeps saying, with increasing bewilderment, "Enough for what?"

That matters because self-imposed guilt can feel every bit as heavy as criticism from someone else. It turns ordinary days into performance reviews. It makes rest feel suspicious. It makes recovery feel lazy. And it makes the retiree harsher on themselves than anyone else in the house is being.

A useful question here is not "What should I be doing now that I am retired?" but "Who decided that, and do I actually agree?" Sometimes the answer is old gender expectations, old work habits, inherited ideas about usefulness, or a private fantasy that retirement would instantly transform you into someone calmer, tidier, and more domestically competent.

Retirement does not require you to become a better exhibit of household virtue. It requires you to build a life that fits the people actually living in the house. That may include more help, more cooking, more chores, or better routines. But it does not require performing a version of retirement that nobody asked for.

When the Pressure Starts Coming from You

Once that script takes hold, it can start to sound less like an idea and more like a moral obligation.

If I am home now, I should be doing more.

If I did not get much done today, I have wasted the day.

If my working partner is still doing the dinner cooking, I am somehow failing retirement and adulthood simultaneously.

This is especially common when the old household arrangement already had established roles. Perhaps your partner did most of the cooking. Perhaps they always have. Perhaps you quietly assumed that once you retired, the balance would naturally shift. Or perhaps you have spent years feeling as though you should have been doing more, and retirement simply turns up the volume on that old guilt.

But that logic deserves to be challenged.

Being retired does not mean you have suddenly become the unpaid household improvements department. It does not mean your worth is now measured in folded laundry, mower lines, repaired hinges, or whether there is something simmering by 6 p.m. It certainly does not mean your partner's longstanding preferences and habits have been magically revoked because you no longer commute.

In those situations, the renegotiation is not just between two people. It is also between the retiree and their own assumptions about usefulness, worth, and what counts as a productive day.

When the Pressure Really Is Coming from Your Partner

Sometimes the pressure is self-imposed. Sometimes it is not.

Sometimes the partner really *is* sending the message that now that you are home, you should be doing more — more chores, more errands, more household management, more visible proof that your day was productive. Sometimes it is said directly. Sometimes it arrives through tone, expectation, or a running commentary on what has not been done.

If that is what is happening, the issue is no longer just internal guilt. It is a real mismatch in expectations, and it needs to be named as such.

That conversation may sound like this: "I am happy to rethink how we divide things now that retirement has changed the shape of the week. But I do not want us to slide into assumptions that being home automatically means I now carry everything."

Retirement may change how household work is divided. But any shift still needs to be discussed, not silently assigned.

When Your Partner Is Not the Source of the Pressure

Sometimes the most helpful thing a partner can say is the simplest: "Why?" followed closely by "No, you do not need to do more stuff."

And sometimes that is exactly the sentence the newly retired person needs to hear most.

In fact, the partner may still be perfectly happy to cook. They may still not care in the slightest that the house is not visitor-ready on a Tuesday. They may be quite sincere when they say, "I never cared before, and I do not care now." The retiree, meanwhile, may still feel as though being home more should automatically translate into becoming more useful, more domestic, and more visibly productive.

There is another version of this story, and it deserves some room too. Not every retirement renegotiation becomes a conflict. Sometimes it looks more like one person quietly panicking that they are not doing enough, while the other keeps offering kindness, perspective, and the occasional reminder that retirement is not something you have to earn every day.

Me: I feel as if I got nothing done today.

Why do you think you have to get more done?

I keep thinking I should be doing more around the house, since I'm home.

You do plenty. You don't have to earn your place here. You're allowed to be retired.

But you are still doing all the cooking when you get home from work. You've been working all day.

That's because I like cooking. It helps me unwind. I don't want to give it up.

That kind of support matters. It does not magically erase the guilt, but it can help expose it for what it is: not a fact, not a moral failure, and not evidence that you are doing retirement incorrectly. Just an inherited script that may no longer deserve authority.

A supportive partner cannot do the adjustment for you. But they can steady it by refusing to join in with the false logic that retirement should now resemble a domestic productivity contest with decorative throw cushions. They can remind you that recovery is not laziness, that rest is not a moral risk, and that being home does not mean your value now depends on whether the guest bathroom is permanently staged like a boutique hotel.

Sometimes the partner is not the problem. They are the antidote to it.

Retirement also changes your wider social life, often more than people expect. Work may have been doing more of the connecting than you realized. Studies of social networks around retirement suggest that some ties change after retirement, especially more peripheral ties and contact with former coworkers.[28, 29] That does not mean your social life disappears; it means some of the connection work that used to happen automatically may now need a little more intention.

Where This Leaves You

Retirement does not arrive with an instruction manual for your relationship or your household. It arrives with good intentions, vague hopes, and the quiet assumption that everything will somehow work itself out. Then someone starts reorganizing the kitchen, someone needs silence for a meeting, or someone realizes that "more time together" is not quite as simple as it sounded.

What this chapter has tried to show is that the friction is not a verdict on your relationship. It is a sign that the house rules need updating.

Noah and his partner did not become retirement experts overnight. They simply began to understand what they were really negotiating — time, space, usefulness, autonomy, and whose rhythm got to shape the day. Once they named that, the house felt less like a battleground and more like a shared adjustment.

That is the work from here. Talk before resentment starts writing the script. Be honest about how much togetherness feels good and how much space you need. Notice whether the pressure to be useful is coming from your partner, from you, or from some old idea that no longer deserves authority. Then make the new rules visible.

Retirement is not just something that happens to one person. It changes the household. It changes the rhythm. It changes the assumptions that used to run quietly in the background. The aim is not to get every rule right the first time. It is to keep talking, keep adjusting, and build a retirement that fits the people actually living in the house.

So, sit down with your partner or household and ask what has changed, what needs to change, and what each of you needs to protect your sanity, your autonomy, and your relationship. Do it with curiosity, not blame. And do it before the blender becomes a legal matter.

What to Take With You

Retirement changes the house rules. More time at home can create friction even in strong relationships, especially if routines, space, and expectations have not been renegotiated.

Constant togetherness is not automatically closeness. Many couples need both shared time and breathing room.

Not all retirement pressure comes from your partner. Some of it comes from your own assumptions about usefulness, productivity, and what being home is supposed to look like.

Questions Worth Asking

What assumptions am I making about how much time together should feel good in retirement, and have I actually said those assumptions out loud?

What expectations am I carrying about usefulness, household roles, or what a "good" retired day should look like — and do I actually agree with them now?

Try This Before You Move On — The House Rules Conversation

Set aside 20 minutes with your partner or household and talk through four things:

- what each of you needs from the day in terms of quiet, space, and routine
- what time you want, and what separate time you need
- what house rules no longer fit now that retirement has changed the rhythm
- what one small change would make the week feel easier for both of you

Write down three practical agreements. Keep them simple. You are not drafting a peace treaty. You are just making the new rules visible.

Chapter 8

The Retirement Rehearsal — How to Test-Drive Your Next Chapter

Olivia had circled her retirement date on her calendar three times, changed it twice, and still woke up at three in the morning wondering if she was making a catastrophic mistake. The problem was not that she had avoided thinking about retirement. She had thought about almost nothing else for eight months. The problem was that imagining retirement and living it are not the same thing.

That is where a rehearsal helps.

Not a performance. Not a full dress production with lighting, costumes, and a tasteful commemorative program. A rehearsal in the ordinary sense — trying something before you commit to it fully. You test-drive the car before you buy it. You try on the shoes before you walk out of the shop. Retirement deserves at least that much courtesy.

A retirement rehearsal is a structured experiment. It might involve extended leave, a trial budget, a temporary reduction in hours, or testing one part of your imagined retirement before you hand in your resignation and hope for the best. The goal is not to prove that retirement will be perfect. The goal is to gather enough real information to make a better decision.

This chapter will help you design a rehearsal that fits your circumstances, notice what it teaches you, and use what you learn to adjust your landing plan. If you have been circling your retirement date, changing it, second-guessing it, and waking up at three in the morning, this chapter is for you. The best way to stop wondering is to try it out. Not forever. Just long enough to know.

Get Your Ducks in a Row Before You Set Them Free: Numbers, Paperwork, and the Basics

Before you can rehearse retirement in any useful way, you need to know what you are rehearsing with. That means getting a basic grip on your numbers and your paperwork. Not perfect. Not comprehensive. Just enough to make the experiment realistic.

Think of this as the pre-flight check. You do not need to rebuild the engine, but you do need to know whether there is fuel in the tank and whether the landing gear works. Otherwise, your rehearsal will tell you nothing useful, because you will spend the whole time worrying about things you could have sorted out beforehand.

This is not the full financial planning process. That comes later, especially if your money situation is complex or you need advice about pension, superannuation, tax, benefits, or investment choices. This is the minimum viable information you need to test-drive retirement without flying blind.

The Few Numbers That Actually Matter Right Now

For the purpose of a rehearsal, you do not need a 30-year financial forecast. You need three working estimates: what is coming in, what is going out, and what the gap looks like.

Start with income. What will you actually have to live on if you retire? This includes your pension, if you have one, superannuation or retirement savings, any government benefits for which you are eligible, and any other income sources that will continue.[17, 30] You do not need precise figures down to the dollar. You need a realistic monthly estimate.

Next, expenses. What does it actually cost you to live right now? Not what you think it should cost. Not what you wish it would cost. What are the basics, and what might change once work is no longer shaping your days, your transport, your meals, your wardrobe, and your incidental spending?

Then look at the gap. For rehearsal purposes, ask what would happen if you lived on that likely retirement income for a few weeks or months. Do you feel fine? Slightly constrained? Constantly annoyed? Do the numbers hold, or do they expose pressure points you had not noticed before?

The point is not to master every financial variable. It is to make the rehearsal credible enough that what you learn from it reflects real life rather than a pleasant fiction.

Paperwork You Will Be Glad You Gathered Early

There is also paperwork. Not mountains of it, but enough that leaving it until the last minute will cause unnecessary stress. A rehearsal is a good time to start gathering what you will need.

Make a list of the documents you will need to access or update when you retire.[17, 30] This typically includes:

- pension statements
- superannuation or retirement savings
- bank and investment account details
- insurance policies (health, life, income protection)
- tax records from the past few years
- mortgage or loan documents
- wills and powers of attorney

You do not need to action all of this right now. But you do need to know where it is, whether it is current, and whether there are any obvious gaps. If your will was written in 1998 and names people who are no longer in your life, that is worth knowing before you retire. If your retirement savings are scattered across four different funds you forgot about, now is the time to find them, list them, and seek advice before deciding whether consolidation makes sense.

The goal is not perfection. The goal is to remove the low-level anxiety that comes from knowing you have left important things undone.

What This Groundwork Actually Buys You

Getting your basic numbers and paperwork sorted does two things. First, it makes your rehearsal more realistic. You can test your retirement budget properly because you know what it is.[16, 17, 30] You can assess whether your spending assumptions hold because you have actual data, not guesses.

Second, it reduces the fear. Much of the anxiety around retirement is not about the decision itself. It is about the unknown. When you know your numbers, even roughly, the fear becomes easier to name. And once you can name it, you can work with it. Concrete information is far easier to work with than getting yourself into a panic at three in the morning.

You do not need to have everything figured out before you start your rehearsal. But you do need to have enough figured out that the rehearsal can teach you something useful. That is what this groundwork is for.

Try Before You Fly: Designing a Retirement Rehearsal That Tells You Something Useful

Once you have your basic numbers sorted and your paperwork gathered, you can design a rehearsal that actually teaches you something. The goal is not to create a perfect simulation of retirement. The goal is to create enough friction with reality that you learn what needs adjusting.

For this chapter, a useful rehearsal has three elements: it should feel close enough to real life to teach you something, last long enough for the novelty to wear off, and give you specific things to watch for. Without those three elements, you are not rehearsing. You are just taking a holiday and calling it research.

What to Simulate (And How to Do It Without Quitting Your Job)

The simplest rehearsal is extended leave. If you can take three to four weeks off work, that may give you enough time to move beyond the first rush of relief and start noticing what ordinary retirement days might feel like. Not a holiday. Not a trip somewhere. Just regular life, without work.

During that time, live as if you have already retired. Do not check work emails. Do not plan a dramatic return. Structure your days the way you imagine retirement days would be structured, and see what happens.

If extended leave is not possible, try a smaller version. If your workplace allows it, reduce your hours temporarily and notice what changes. Work four days a week instead of five. See what you do with the extra day. See whether it feels like freedom or like a gap you do not know how to fill.

Another option is to simulate your retirement budget while you are still earning. For one or two months, live on what your retirement income would actually be.[17, 30] Put the difference into savings or a separate account. See whether the budget holds. See where the pressure points are. See what you miss and what you do not.

You can also test specific elements of your retirement plan separately. If you think volunteering will give your week structure, try it. If you imagine yourself happily pottering at home, see how three ordinary weekdays of that actually feel. If you think a slower pace will suit you beautifully, try giving yourself one and notice whether you relax into it or start reorganizing the pantry out of existential necessity.

What to Watch for While the Rehearsal Is Happening

The point of a rehearsal is not simply to get through it. It is to pay attention.

For this rehearsal, pay attention to the things most likely to shape daily life: your energy, your time, your spending, and your relationships. Do you feel more settled without work, or strangely flat? Do the days feel spacious, or do they stretch out in ways that leave you slightly adrift at sea? Do you spend less than expected, more than expected, or just differently? Does being home more improve things, expose fault lines, or simply require some renegotiation?

Also pay attention to what you miss. Do you miss the work itself, the routine, the social contact, the status, or simply the built-in reason to leave the house?[31] Missing something is not a sign that retirement is a mistake. It is a clue about what your next chapter needs to contain.

Likewise, notice what feels unexpectedly good. The slower mornings. The reduced irritability. The absence of Sunday dread. The return of energy you had forgotten was possible. These are clues too.

The aim is not to produce a verdict after one odd Tuesday. It is to gather patterns. A good rehearsal gives you less fantasy and more evidence.

How to Interpret What You Learn

When Olivia reviewed her rehearsal, what surprised her most was not that some parts had worked and others had not. It was that the uncertainty had changed shape. She was no longer guessing in the dark. She was working with information.

When the rehearsal ends, resist the urge to reduce it to one dramatic conclusion. *"It was amazing; therefore, I am ready,"* or *"I felt restless on day six, therefore retirement will ruin my life."* Neither of those is particularly useful. Instead, ask better questions.

- What felt easier than expected?
- What felt harder?
- What did you miss?
- What did you not miss at all?
- What parts of your retirement fantasy held up in real life, and which ones looked better in your imagination?
- What practical adjustments would make retirement work better?

Sometimes the rehearsal confirms that you are ready. Sometimes it shows you that you need more structure, more savings, more social contact, or a bridge plan rather than a full stop. That is not a verdict on retirement. It is information about the version of retirement that might actually work for you. Sometimes it tells you that the issue is not retirement itself, but the need to design it more honestly.

That is not disappointing. That is useful.

A rehearsal that reveals something unexpected has not gone badly. It has done its job.

Where This Leaves You

A retirement rehearsal is not about proving that retirement will be perfect. It is about finding out what needs adjusting while there is still room to adjust it.

Olivia went back to work without perfect certainty, but with something better than another month of three-in-the-morning panic. She had evidence. She knew which parts of her imagined retirement held up, which parts needed more thought, and which parts had looked much better in theory than they felt in ordinary life.

That is the gift of rehearsal. It turns vague worry into useful information. You may discover that you need more structure than you expected, or less. You may find that your budget needs work, your social life needs attention, or your fantasy of endless unstructured time loses its sparkle by Wednesday afternoon. None of that means retirement is wrong. It means your plan is getting more honest.

Not everyone will have the option to rehearse in advance. Some people retire suddenly and have to work things out in real time. If that is you, the same principles still apply: track what happens, notice your patterns, and adjust as you go.

But if you can rehearse — through leave, reduced hours, a trial budget, or a smaller test of the life you imagine — take the opportunity. The rehearsal is not the decision. It is the information that helps you make the decision well.

So, stop trying to solve retirement entirely in your head. Give yourself a way to test it. Watch what happens. Write it down. Adjust the plan.

Then, when the time comes to retire, you will not be leaping into a fantasy. You will be stepping into something you have already begun to understand.

What to Take With You

Thinking about retirement and living it are not the same thing. A rehearsal helps close that gap before the stakes get higher.

A useful rehearsal is realistic enough to reveal pressure points — money, structure, identity, routine, and relationships — while you still have room to adjust.

The goal is not to prove retirement will be perfect. The goal is to gather real information that helps you build a plan that fits your actual life.

Questions Worth Asking

Which part of retirement feels most uncertain to me right now — the money, the structure of the days, the loss of work identity, or something else — and how could I test that rather than just worry about it?

If I had three to four weeks to live as if I were already retired, what would I most want to learn from the experience?

Try This Before You Move On — Design Your Retirement Rehearsal

Choose one way to rehearse retirement in the next three months.

It might be:

- taking extended leave and living an ordinary life without work
- reducing your hours temporarily
- trialing your retirement budget for one or two months
- testing one specific part of your retirement plan, such as volunteering, slower mornings, or spending more time at home

Then write down:

- what you will simulate
- how long you will do it
- what you will watch for
- what would count as a useful insight, even if it is not the one you hoped for

Keep it simple. This is not about creating a flawless experiment. It is about learning something real before you make the final call.

Chapter 9

The Retirement Countdown — What to Do Before You Walk Out the Door

Millie had submitted her retirement notice three months earlier, and everyone kept asking if she was excited. The honest answer — which she did not say out loud — was that she felt less excited and more like she was standing at the edge of a diving board, trying to remember whether she had actually checked that there was water in the pool.

The decision itself no longer worried her. What worried her was the space between deciding and leaving. That strange in-between stretch when you are still employed, already imagining retirement, and quietly wondering whether something important is about to slip through the cracks.

This is the chapter for that stretch.

Making the decision to retire is one thing. Getting yourself out the door with the essentials handled is another. Your workplace may give you a form to fill out, a farewell morning tea, and perhaps an exit interview if everyone is feeling ambitious. But the real work of leaving well usually sits elsewhere — in the quiet sorting, checking, asking, deciding, and talking that happens before the last day arrives.

The aim is not to create a flawless exit. If you are looking for perfection, you may wish to consult someone with a clipboard, a laminator, and no remaining emotional life. The aim here is simpler - to leave with enough clarity that your first weeks of retirement are not spent frantically solving big problems that could have been smaller problems earlier.

Some people approach this countdown with military precision. Spreadsheets. Timelines. Color-coded folders. If that is you, excellent. Please enjoy your tabs. But if you are tired, distracted, overloaded, or quietly hoping the whole thing will somehow organize itself, this chapter will help you work out what needs attention before you go and what can safely wait.

You do not need to have everything sorted. You need to have enough sorted. Enough to make the landing steadier. Enough to reduce the avoidable surprises. Enough to walk out the door with a reasonable sense that you have not left your future self holding a bag of administrative snakes.

If you have already made the decision to retire, this chapter is your bridge between "I am going" and "I have gone." It will not remove every uncertainty. But it will help you step off the edge with a little more footing beneath you.

And frankly, at this point, footing may be more useful than excitement.

The Paperwork Before the Peace: What to Sort Now, What Can Wait

Retirement paperwork has a special talent for feeling both urgent and boring at the same time. It is the administrative equivalent of packing for a long trip — you know you need to do it, you know forgetting something important will cause problems later, but the actual process makes you want to lie down and think about it tomorrow.

The good news is that not all paperwork is created equal. Some of it genuinely needs your attention before you walk out the door. Some of it can wait until you have actually retired and have had a chance to catch your breath. Some of it is optional busy work that you can ignore entirely without consequence. The trick is knowing the difference.

At the top of the list are the things that affect income, access, insurance, and legal protection. Pension choices. Retirement fund applications. Health insurance. Bank details. Your will. Powers of attorney. Beneficiary nominations. These are not glamorous tasks, but they are the ones most likely to create headaches if left dangling.

What matters here is not that you complete everything in one heroic weekend. It is that you identify the paperwork that has consequences and deal with that first. The rest can wait until your brain is functioning at something above mild alarm.

The Conversations That Matter More Than You Think

Paperwork is not the only thing people postpone. Conversations get pushed aside too — partly because they are awkward, and partly because they make retirement feel more real.

You need to tell work you are leaving in a way that protects your relationships and your boundaries. You need to talk to your partner about what retirement will actually mean in practical terms, not just in the glossy brochure version where everyone is delighted and beautifully rested. You may need to talk to adult children, ageing parents, or anyone else whose assumptions about your availability are about to change. And, at some point, you will need a tolerable answer to the question, *"So what will you do now?"* because people will ask it with more enthusiasm than tact.

These conversations do not need to be perfect. They just need to happen before silence creates problems that are harder to fix later.

The goal is clarity, not performance. You are not asking for permission. You are managing expectations, protecting your relationships, and giving the people around you a more realistic sense of what comes next.

The Last 90 Days: — How to Leave with a Plan, Not a Panic

The final stretch before retirement is not a countdown to freedom so much as a countdown to a different kind of work — the work of making sure you do not walk out the door and immediately realize you have forgotten something that will cost you money, time, or peace of mind.

Official retirement guidance from many countries, such as the United States, the United Kingdom, and Australia, tends to circle around the same practical tasks — estimating retirement income, checking retirement funds, pension or superannuation options, understanding benefits, reviewing spending, and making key decisions early enough to change course if needed.[30. 32, 33, 34]

Useful Official Retirement Planning Guides

United States

Social Security Administration — Your Retirement Checklist. https://www.ssa.gov/pubs/EN-05-10377.pdf

U.S. Department of Labor — Retirement Toolkit. https://www.dol.gov/sites/dolgov/files/ebsa/about-ebsa/our-activities/resource-center/publications/retirement-toolkit.pdf

Australia

Moneysmart — Retirement Planning Checklist. https://static.moneysmart.gov.au/ms2026/campaign/retirement/Retirement-planning-checklist.pdf

United Kingdom

MoneyHelper — Work Out How Much You Will Need in Retirement. https://www.moneyhelper.org.uk/content/dam/maps/en/pensions/moneyhelper-retirement-budgeting-leaflet.pdf

Retirement rules vary depending on where you live, who you worked for, and the pension, superannuation, or benefits system you belong to. Official guides are helpful, but they cannot know the unique little details of your actual life.

Before making decisions about retirement income, pension or superannuation options, tax, health cover, government benefits, or estate planning, talk to someone qualified to help you make informed choices. That might be a financial adviser, a pension, retirement or superannuation fund adviser, an HR retirement specialist, a government benefits officer, an accountant, a solicitor, or another professional who understands the systems with which you are dealing.

The simplest way to approach these final months is to break them into phases. Not because life will obediently follow your timeline, but because phased thinking stops the whole thing becoming one giant, noisy pile of tasks in your head. To make the countdown manageable, this chapter uses a simple 90-60-30 framework.

The 90-60-30 Framework

The 90-60-30 framework is not a rigid system. It is a way to sort decisions into what matters now, what matters next, and what can wait until closer to the finish line. If you are already inside the final month, all is not lost. You have just compressed the timeline. Focus on what has consequences and let the rest be less dramatic than it wants to be.

For Millie, the countdown became less intimidating once it stopped being one giant blur of "things I might be forgetting" and turned into phases. She still had plenty to do, but it no longer all lived in her head at once.

At 90 Days — The Big Picture

This is when you deal with decisions that have deadlines, long lead times, or consequences if they are left too late.

Submit any formal retirement application, resignation notice, pension paperwork, superannuation forms, or benefit claims required by your employer, pension fund, superannuation provider, or retirement system. Some schemes have strict filing windows; others are more flexible. Check the rules that apply to you and give yourself enough time to correct errors, provide missing documents, or confirm your retirement date.[30, 32, 33, 34]

If you have a defined benefit pension, lifetime income option, annuity, pension drawdown arrangement, or other structured retirement income product, this is also the time to understand your choices.

Some decisions become difficult, costly, or impossible to change after retirement begins, especially where survivor benefits, lump sums, drawdown options, or lifetime payments are involved. Do not leave those decisions to the final week, when your brain is already full of farewell speeches, password resets, and the emotional weight of cleaning out your desk.

If your retirement income depends on years of service, contribution history, employment credits, earnings records, or eligibility rules, ask for a statement or estimate and check it carefully. Errors are usually easier to query before retirement than after payments begin.

This is also the right time to step back and look at the whole landing picture. What absolutely has to be in place before your last day? What conversations still need to happen? What financial loose ends are likely to make the first month bumpier than it needs to be? The point at 90 days is not detail. It is making sure the big pieces are on the board.

At 60 Days — The Money and the Admin

This is when you turn the big picture into something more concrete.

By now, you want a rough but honest sense of what is coming in, what is going out, and where the pressure points are likely to be. If you have not done that work yet, do not panic. Do it now. Confirm what income will actually be available in the first few months, what bills are still due, and what needs updating before the pay cheque stops. Official retirement planning guidance commonly recommends estimating retirement income, reviewing likely spending, checking pension or superannuation options, and making sure you understand how your retirement income will actually work in practice.1[7, 30, 33, 34]

This is also the time to review any insurance, benefits, memberships or income protections tied to your employment. Also, review your work phone, work email, salary packaging, employee discounts, or any other benefits on which you may have quietly been relying. If work has been carrying more of your financial and administrative life than you realized, this is where that becomes visible.

You should also check your will, powers of attorney, beneficiary nominations, and any advance health documents that apply in your jurisdiction. These are not dramatic retirement tasks, but they are deeply sensible ones. They are far easier to sort before the transition than in the middle of it.[35] Treat this as a practical review, not a dramatic confrontation with mortality. You are not summoning the Grim Reaper. You are making sure the paperwork knows what it is supposed to do.

At 30 Days — The Practical and the Relational

This is when the countdown starts to feel real.

At this point, you are dealing with work accounts, handover, passwords and access issues, practical loose ends, and the conversations that shape the landing. What happens to your email? Your files? Your devices? Your passwords? What do you need to save, transfer, return, or let go of? What unfinished work genuinely matters, and what can be left without guilt?

This is also the time to talk properly with your partner, household, or close family about what the first few weeks might look like. Not in broad, cheerful terms. In actual terms. Who will be home, when, and doing what? How much routine do you want? How much space do you need? What assumptions are floating around unspoken that would be better dealt with now rather than after someone has quietly redesigned the kitchen and called it helpful?

At 30 days, practicalities and relationships start to overlap. That is normal. Retirement is not just an administrative change. It is emotional and domestic and financial and social and logistical, all at once. Research on couples adjusting to retirement also shows that retirement is not experienced only as an individual transition; it affects household rhythms, emotional adjustment, and relationship dynamics too.[24] The aim is not to control every detail. It is to reduce the number of avoidable surprises waiting for you on the other side of your last day.

In the Final Week — Keep It Small

The last week before retirement is not the time for heroic new projects. It is the time to keep things simple.

Confirm the essentials. Check the paperwork one last time. Make sure you know what happens to pay, leave, access, and insurance. Tie up what truly needs tying up. Let go of what is not yours to carry into retirement. If there is an urge to solve everything in one final burst of competence, ignore it. That path can lead to stress and mediocre decisions.

The final week is for leaving with enough done — not for proving you can execute a flawless exit while emotionally overloaded. That was never the assignment.

Where This Leaves You

The retirement countdown is not a test. It is a bridge between two versions of your life, and bridges do not require perfection. They require enough stability to get you safely across.

Millie was not floating toward retirement on a cloud of serenity. But she was no longer standing at the edge hoping for the best, either. She had a plan, a timeline, and a clearer sense of what needed attention before she walked out the door. That did not make the transition effortless. It made it less mysterious.

That is the real work of this chapter. Not to turn retirement into a project-management exercise, and not to squeeze every loose end into the final weeks of work. The point is to notice what matters, deal with what has consequences, and stop carrying the whole countdown around in your head as one giant blur of possible disasters.

Some tasks will feel tedious. Some conversations will feel awkward. Some decisions will require advice from people who understand the systems you are dealing with. None of that means you are doing retirement badly. It means you are moving through a real transition, with real paperwork, real relationships, real money, and real feelings attached.

The 90-60-30 framework is only a guide. Use it to create shape, not pressure. If you have three months, spread the work out. If you have four weeks, focus on what has consequences. If you have already missed a few neat little milestones, all is not lost. Start where you are, sort what matters most, and let the rest wait its turn.

Leaving well does not mean leaving perfectly. It means leaving with enough handled that you can begin the next stage without spending the first month chasing avoidable problems. It means having the necessary conversations before silence becomes confusing. It means giving your future self a softer landing.

You are not standing at the edge of a diving board hoping there is water in the pool. You are standing there with a reasonable sense that the pool is there, the water is deep enough, and you have done what you can to make the landing steadier.

That is not certainty.

But it is enough.

And enough, as it turns out, is exactly what you need to jump.

What to Take With You

The period between deciding to retire and actually leaving work needs its own plan. The goal is not to have everything sorted, but to have the things that matter most handled.

The 90-60-30 framework helps break the countdown into manageable phases so you can focus on what matters now, what matters next, and what can wait.

The most important pre-retirement tasks are usually not glamorous — paperwork, money, access, and conversations — but they are the ones that make the landing steadier.

Questions Worth Asking

Which part of the countdown am I most tempted to avoid — the paperwork, the conversations, the budget, or the practical loose ends — and what makes that part harder than it needs to be?

If I had to focus on only four things before my last day, what would make the biggest difference to how steady the first month of retirement feels?

Try This Before You Move On — The 90-60-30 Countdown List

Draw three columns and label them **90 Days**, **60 Days**, and **30 Days**.

Under each heading, list what needs to be handled in that phase. Include:

- paperwork that affects income or access

- insurance or legal updates
- conversations with partner, family, or work
- budget or cashflow checks
- practical loose ends that will matter in the first month

Then mark each item:

- **Must do** before last day
- **Should do** if possible
- **Can wait** until after retirement

Do not aim for beauty. Aim for visibility. The point is to see the countdown clearly enough that you can stop carrying it all in your head.

Chapter 10

Better Late Than Never — The Checklist for What Comes Next

Mei had been retired for four months when she finally admitted to herself that she had no idea what she was doing. She had left work with relief, exhaustion, and a vague plan to "figure it out as she went," but the figuring-it-out part was not happening, and her days were starting to feel like they were happening *to* her rather than the other way around.

If you are reading this chapter, there is a reasonable chance you fall into one of three camps. The first — you have been retired for a while, and you are starting to suspect you skipped some steps. The second — you are about to retire and you have just realized you have not actually prepared for much beyond your last day at work. The third — you read the earlier chapters, nodded along, and then life happened and you retired anyway without doing half the things you meant to do.

All three are normal.

Retirement does not always arrive with a neat plan, a tidy folder of paperwork, and a serene sense of readiness. Sometimes it arrives with exhaustion, relief, and a strong desire to stop thinking about work for at least six weeks. Sometimes you leave because you have to, not because you are ready. Sometimes you do all the thinking and none of the doing, and then you are retired and staring at a Tuesday morning with no structure and a growing sense that you may have overlooked something important.

This chapter is for anyone who has already crossed the line into retirement and is now looking around, wondering what they were supposed to have done by now. It is for the people who skipped the landing plan because they were too tired to make one. For the people who meant to sort out their retirement fund, their budget, their routines, and their sense of purpose, but somehow never got around to it. For the people who are four months in, or eight months in, or a year in, and have just realized they are drifting.

The good news is that it is not too late. You have not ruined your future. You have just started in a different order than the books assume you will. And that is fixable.

What this chapter will do is help you with triage. Not in a dramatic, emergency room sense. In a practical, "let us work out what actually needs attention right now" sense. It will help you identify the administrative, financial, and practical gaps that matter most, close the ones that need closing, and let go of the ones that do not.

You do not need to go back and do everything perfectly. You just need to do enough to stop drifting and start steering.

This chapter will walk you through a catch-up checklist that covers the essentials — the paperwork you may have missed, the money questions you have been avoiding, the routines you have not yet built, and the small decisions that will help you regain a sense of control. It will also help you recognize what does not need fixing — because not every gap is a crisis, and not every imperfect start needs correcting.

If you have been feeling behind, anxious, or quietly ashamed that you did not prepare better, this chapter is your permission to stop going round in circles and start building. Retirement is not a performance. It is a transition. And transitions can be messy or late, and still turn out fine.

You are not starting from scratch. You are starting from here. And here is a perfectly reasonable place to begin.

Already Retired and Slightly Adrift? Start Here

If you are reading this section, chances are you have already retired and you are now realizing that you may have skipped a few steps. Or perhaps you retired in a rush — health crisis, redundancy, or sheer exhaustion — and there was no time for a neat landing plan. Or maybe you did think about it, nodded along to all the sensible advice, and then life happened and you found yourself retired anyway, with a vague sense that you were supposed to have done more preparation than you actually did.

None of this means you did retirement wrong. It just means you started in a different order.

The truth is, not everyone crosses into retirement with a color-coded checklist, a tidy folder of paperwork, and a serene sense of readiness. Some people leave because they have to. Some leave because they are too tired to think straight. Some leave with every intention of "sorting it all out later," and then later becomes four months, and the sorting has not happened, and the days are starting to feel like they are happening to you rather than the other way around.

If that sounds familiar, this section is for you.

What Drift Actually Feels Like

Drift is not the same as depression, though it can feel adjacent. It is more like a low-grade sense of aimlessness. You wake up without a clear reason to get up. You fill your days, but nothing feels particularly meaningful.

You are not miserable, exactly. You are just... unsettled.

Research on retirement adjustment suggests that the unsettling feeling many new retirees describe is not simply boredom or ingratitude. It often reflects the sudden loss of a life structure — the roles, routines, relationships, activities, and places that once gave ordinary days their shape.[36] Work does not only provide income; it organizes time, supplies routines, creates regular contact with other people, and offers a ready-made sense of usefulness.[31]

When that structure disappears, even people who wanted to retire can feel strangely loose in their own lives. Researchers describe retirement as a process in which the self and the person's "life structure" have to be rebuilt together — roles, relationships, activities, groups, places, and routines all need to find a new arrangement.[36] Furthermore, retirement is framed as a period of major change and instability that can challenge a person's sense of meaning.[37] In that light, drift is not a personal defect. It is the awkward middle stage between the old structure that has fallen away and the new one that has not yet taken shape.

Drift does not always feel dramatic. It often feels like a low-level fog. You may be drifting if your days have started to blur together, not because they are peaceful, but because they no longer have much shape. The days start slipping past without much distinction. You are not miserable, exactly, but you are not quite engaged either. You forget what day it is, lose the rhythm of ordinary routines, and find yourself filling time rather than using it.

You may have plenty to do, but no real sense of direction. You may be relieved to be away from work, but still strangely restless without the structure it once provided. That is drift — not disaster, not failure, just the uncomfortable feeling of being temporarily without your usual bearings. This is not a character flaw. It is a predictable response to the sudden absence of structure, identity, and daily purpose that work provided.

The good news is that drift is often temporary. It responds well to small, practical steps that restore structure, social connection, and a sense of agency. You do not need a grand reinvention. You just need to stop floating and start steering.[38, 39]

The Triage Question — What Actually Needs Attention Right Now?

When you are already retired and feeling adrift, the temptation is to panic and try to fix everything at once.

Sort the money. Set up a perfect routine. Declutter the house. Reconnect socially. Start Pilates. Learn Italian. Become a person who meal preps.

This is not the moment for that - so do not do that. It will overwhelm you, and you will end up doing nothing. Instead, ask yourself one simple question — *What is the one thing that, if I sorted it out this week, would make me feel more in control?*

Not eventually. Not ideally. Not in the fantasy version of retirement where you become composed, energetic, and strangely fond of chia seeds. This week.

Whatever it is, that is your starting point. The key is to stop treating every unfinished thing as if it needs attention right now.

The Three-Bucket Triage System

For Mei, the shift began when she stopped treating every unfinished thing as a sign she had failed and started sorting them into what needed attention now, what mattered but could wait, and what was merely nagging at her conscience. That was the moment retirement began to feel more manageable.

When life feels unsettled, the trouble is not always that there is too much to do. It is that everything starts to seem as though it needs attention right now. A bit of paperwork, a money worry, the fact that you have not exercised in weeks, the strange flatness of your days, that cupboard you still have not sorted — all of it turns up at once and starts waving for attention. That is when people either panic, avoid, or waste precious energy trying to fix the wrong thing first. In an emergency department, triage exists for exactly this reason — to sort what needs immediate attention from what can safely wait. Retirement may not involve a waiting room or a blood pressure cuff, but the principle still holds.

The Three-Bucket Triage System is simply a way of sorting your concerns into three groups: things that need attention now, things that matter but are not urgent, and things that would be nice to deal with but can safely wait. It is not about becoming ruthlessly efficient or turning retirement into a project plan. It is about reducing overwhelm, making better decisions, and using your energy where it will make the most difference. Once you can see what belongs in each bucket, it becomes much easier to stop getting stuck and start moving.

Bucket One: Urgent and Practical

The buckets work best when you are honest about consequences, not just feelings. A task may feel urgent because it is irritating, embarrassing, or has been sitting there too long, but the real question is whether anything significant happens if you leave it another week.

This is the bucket for things that have consequences if you keep ignoring them.

Examples include:

- not knowing when your income is landing
- not understanding your current spending
- an unresolved health insurance issue
- paperwork that affects access to money or services
- bills or legal matters that genuinely need attention

These tasks are rarely exciting, but they are stabilizing. They are the retirement equivalent of fixing the loose railing before repainting the guest room.

Bucket Two: Important but Not Urgent

Once the immediate pressure points are under control, this is where you begin rebuilding the shape of ordinary life.

This bucket includes the things that matter for your quality of life but do not have to be solved by Friday.

Examples include:

- building a weekly rhythm
- reconnecting socially
- adding exercise back in to your life
- reviewing what gives your days shape or purpose
- making the housework better for the life you are now living

These things matter a great deal, but they can be approached steadily. They are built through rhythm, not solved in one heroic burst of misplaced enthusiasm.

Bucket Three: Nice to Have

This is where many of us go when life feels messy, because small visible improvements can feel wonderfully like they can be controlled.

This is the bucket for things that are perfectly lovely but not currently essential.

Examples include:

- color-coding the linen cupboard
- learning pottery
- reorganizing the pantry into matching containers with fancy labels
- becoming the sort of person who has a refined morning ritual involving journalling, herbal tea, and a cushion in a sunbeam

There is nothing wrong with these things. In fact, they may become part of a very satisfying retirement. But if your retirement feels unstable, they are not where you begin.

The point of triage is not to become hyper-efficient. It is to quiet the sense that everything is wrong all at once. Start with one thing from Bucket One — one practical issue that would make life feel steadier if it were handled. Then, when you have a little more room to think, choose one thing from Bucket Two. After that, stop and breathe.

You do not need to fix everything. You just need to stop the drift.

The Catch-Up Checklist — Administrative, Financial, and Practical Gaps to Close

Once you know what bucket things belong in, the next step is practical catch-up — the paperwork you may have missed, the money questions you have been avoiding, the routines you have not yet built, and the small decisions that will help you regain a sense of control.

If you are already retired and realizing you have gaps, the first move is to stop panicking and start sorting. Not everything at once. Not perfectly. Just methodically enough to regain a sense of control.

The point is - you are not starting from scratch. You are starting from here. And *here* is a perfectly reasonable place to begin your practical catch-up checklist. In this book, to make it less overwhelming, we will keep the catch-up checklist simple. It is organized into three broad categories — administrative, financial, and practical. Work through them in order or jump to whichever one is causing you the most anxiety right now. Either approach works.

Administrative Gaps: The Loose Ends You Have Not Yet Tied Up

Administrative tasks are rarely urgent until suddenly they are. If you have been retired for a few months and have not yet dealt with the following, now is the time.

- **Pension, retirement savings or superannuation paperwork** — confirm your payments have started, your account details are correct, and you understand what you are receiving and when. If you have multiple retirement fund accounts, check whether consolidation makes sense.

- **Tax and financial reporting** — work out whether you need to lodge a tax return, update your tax details, or notify the tax office of your change in circumstances. If you left in the middle of a tax year, this matters more than you think.

- **Health insurance and Medicare** — if your health cover was through work, confirm what happens now. Check your Medicare status, any gap cover, and whether you need private health insurance or can manage without it.

- **Forwarding address and contact details** — update your details with banks, retirement funders, insurers, and anyone else who needs to find you. It sounds trivial until you miss an important letter.

- **Beneficiary nominations** — check whether your paperwork still reflects your current wishes. Check that your retirement, insurance, and any other accounts have up-to-date beneficiary details. This is one of those things people forget until it becomes a problem for someone else.

- **Work-related accounts and access** — make sure personal files, contacts, and records are where they need to be.

This is not glamorous, but it is stabilizing. If this list feels overwhelming, pick one item and deal with it this week. Then pick another next week. You do not need to clear the entire list by the end of the day. Every small item you close is one less thing rattling around in your head at three in the morning.

Financial Gaps: The Money Questions You Have Been Avoiding

Money anxiety grows very efficiently in vagueness. If you have been retired for a while and still have only a hazy sense of what is coming in, what is going out, and where the pressure points are, now is the time to look. Money avoidance is common, especially when you are already tired. But financial clarity reduces anxiety faster than almost anything else on this list.

- **Income and expenses** — Work out what money is coming in each month and what is going out. You do not need a complex budget. You just need to know whether you are covering your costs or slowly bleeding savings without noticing.

- **Buffer and emergency fund** — Check whether you have a financial cushion for unexpected costs—car repairs, medical bills, urgent house maintenance. If not, start building one, even if it is small.

- **Spending patterns** — Notice where your money is actually going. Are you spending more on takeaway because you have not built a routine? Are you impulse-buying because you are bored? No judgment. Just awareness.

- **Debt and repayments** — If you have debt, confirm you are managing repayments and that nothing has slipped through the cracks. If repayments are becoming difficult, contact your lender sooner rather than later.

- **Withdrawal strategy** — If you are drawing from savings or super, check that you have a sustainable plan. Random withdrawals without a strategy can deplete funds faster than expected.

Retirement income research suggests that the drawdown stage can be surprisingly difficult. Without a clear plan, many retirees either cling too tightly to their savings because they fear running out or are spending without a reliable sense of what their money needs to cover. A simple withdrawal plan — even a rough one — helps turn a nest egg into usable income, giving you more confidence about what you can spend and when.[40, 41]

You do not need a twelve-tab spreadsheet unless that brings you joy, and frankly, I hope it does not. You need a realistic view of your current position so you can stop imagining that every financial uncertainty is a catastrophe.

Practical Gaps: The Structure You Have Not Yet Built

Many retirement problems are not really problems of *meaning*. They are problems of *rhythm*. These are the everyday gaps that can leave retirement feeling more unsettled than it needs to. If your days have gone floppy around the edges, start small.

- **Routine and structure** — If your days feel shapeless, build a basic weekly rhythm. Set a consistent wake-up time. Create two or three weekly anchor points (an anchor point is a fixed activity that happens at roughly the same time each day or week). Not a rigid schedule. Just enough structure to stop the drift.

- **Social connection** — If you have been isolating, reconnect with one person this week. A coffee. A phone call. Anything that breaks the pattern. Make one regular social contact non-negotiable.

- **Health checks** — Book any overdue medical appointments. Doctor. Dentist. Optometrist. Whatever you have been putting off. Reintroduce movement.

- **Household admin** — Deal with the small tasks that have been nagging at you and making you feel unstable. The broken door handle. The expired car registration. The pile of mail. Choose one useful thing to do each day before lunch. Leave the house more often than strictly necessary.

You are not building a new corporate schedule, and you do not need to fix everything. You are building enough shape that the days stop blurring into one another. You just need to close the gaps that are making you feel unstable. Once those are handled, you can start building forward momentum.

The Small Fixes That Change Everything

People often imagine that getting retirement back on track requires a dramatic reinvention. In reality, the biggest shift usually comes from a few small, boring, surprisingly effective actions done consistently.

One form submitted.

One bill sorted.

One walk taken.

One coffee with a friend booked.

One drawer finally decluttered.

One decision made.

Momentum rarely arrives in a blaze of glory. More often, it turns up quietly after you do the first sensible thing.

Where This Leaves You

Mei sat at her kitchen table three weeks after making her catch-up list, and for the first time in months, retirement felt less like something happening to her and more like something she could shape. She had not fixed everything. She had not become a model retiree with a color-coded calendar, a flawless budget, and a serene sense of purpose before breakfast. But she had closed the gaps that mattered most. She had sorted her retirement funds, updated her health insurance, and built a rough weekly pattern that gave her days more shape. She had stopped berating herself for being behind and started working from where she actually was.

That is what this chapter has been about — not perfection, not catching up to an imaginary standard, and not pretending retirement should fall neatly into place. It is about finding your footing after the fact.

If you are already retired and realizing you skipped some steps, you did not do retirement wrong. You simply began in a different order. And that is fixable. The administrative gaps can be closed. The financial questions can be answered. Routines can be built. You do not need to go back to the beginning. You can begin again from here.

The catch-up checklist is not a test. It is a triage tool — a way of deciding what deserves your attention first. You do not need to complete every item by Friday or emerge as the patron saint of retirement readiness. Start with what matters most now, deal with that, and then move to the next thing. One practical step. One steadier week. One small decision that gives you more room to breathe.

Structure is not about filling every hour or performing productivity. It is about creating enough rhythm that your days feel intentional rather than accidental. A few anchor points, a weekly plan with blank space, and a balance across movement, connection, purpose, and rest can be enough to help you feel less suspended and more grounded.

If you are reading this in the middle of the adjustment, know this — the aimlessness, boredom, guilt about resting, and identity shift can all be part of the transition. It does not mean retirement is going badly. It means your old scaffolding has come down and the new one is still being built. Give yourself time, grace, and permission to course-correct without shame.

Retirement is not a performance. It is a transition. Mei did not retire with a plan. Four months in, she built one. And that made all the difference — not because she did everything right, but because she stopped waiting for retirement to make sense on its own and began giving it shape.

What to Take With You

It is not too late to catch up. A messy or underprepared start does not mean retirement is ruined; it means some practical gaps still need attention.

The most helpful first move is triage — sorting what is urgent, what matters but can wait, and what is optional for later.

Small, practical fixes create momentum. You do not need a grand reinvention. You need enough structure and clarity to stop drifting and start steering.

Questions Worth Asking

What is the one unfinished thing that is making me feel most unsettled right now, and which bucket does it belong in?

If I stopped trying to fix everything at once, what is the first small action that would make this week feel more manageable?

Try This Before You Move On — The Catch-Up Snapshot

Take one sheet of paper and divide it into three sections:

- Urgent and Practical
- Important but Not Urgent
- Nice to Have

Then list everything currently rattling around in your head about retirement — paperwork, money, routines, health, relationships, the lot. Put each item into one of the three sections.

Circle one item from the first section and one item from the second. Ignore the third section for now.

Those two items are your next steps.

Conclusion

You made it! Not just to the end of this book, but to the point where retirement has stopped being a vague someday problem and become something you are looking at directly. That matters. Because asking the question properly — not just letting it rattle around in your head at three in the morning, not just half-joking about wanting out, not just telling yourself you will deal with it later — takes more honesty than most people realize.

If you are reading this, you are probably still tired. You might still be uncertain. You might have more questions now than when you started. That is normal. Retirement is not a single decision you make once and then never think about again. It is a decision, a transition, and then a process of building a life that fits. And each part asks something different of you.

By now, you should have a clearer sense of whether you are looking at a **Leave, Linger**, or **Lighten the Load** situation. You should know which signals are worth paying attention to, which numbers actually matter, and which assumptions need testing before you make the call. You should also know that retirement is not just about money. It is about health, identity, routine, relationships, and the practical business of building a life that no longer revolves around work.

You should also know this — feeling flat, uncertain, a little sad, or slightly disoriented while you are thinking seriously about retirement does not mean you are making a poor decision. It often means you are standing in the middle of a major life transition that our culture barely acknowledges and rarely prepares people for. The awkwardness is not a sign that you are off track. More often, it is a sign that something significant is shifting and you are beginning to face it honestly.

This book was never meant to tell you what to decide. It was meant to help you work out how to decide, and how to land more steadily once you do. That is why it has walked you through the signals that it may be time to stop, the three-path decision framework, the practical realities of involuntary retirement, the money questions, the identity shift, the relationship renegotiations, the rehearsal, the countdown, and the catch-up work that sometimes comes later than planned.

You do not need to have the next ten years mapped out in detail. You do not need a dazzling new identity by next Tuesday. And you do not need to prove, before you even retire, that the next chapter will be beautifully organized, deeply meaningful, and conducted in tasteful linen while learning Portuguese and making sourdough

You need enough clarity to take the next honest step.

That might mean deciding to leave now.

It might mean lingering a little longer and waiting strategically.

It might mean lightening the load by building a bridge plan toward full retirement.

It might mean closing a few practical gaps before you go.

It might mean giving yourself permission to rest before you attempt reinvention.

All of that counts as progress.

If you have already begun retirement, I hope this book has helped you feel less blindsided and less alone. If you are still deciding, I hope it has helped you move from noise to something more useful. Either way, the goal was never perfection. The goal was steadiness.

So, take what is useful. Ignore what is not. Keep the checklist. Revisit the questions. Have the awkward conversations. Do the boring paperwork. Protect your health. And when the time comes, step toward the next chapter in a way that is kinder to your body, calmer for your mind, and more honest about what you need.

You are allowed to want a life that does not require you to run on empty.

You are allowed to stop proving yourself.

And you are allowed to build what comes next, one sensible step at a time.

Go get it!

Enjoyed the Book? Leave a Review

One last thing to do, and this one does not require a spreadsheet, a calculator, or a difficult conversation over dinner.

Reviews help other readers decide whether this book is the right companion for where they are right now.

If this book made you laugh, nod, breathe out, or feel a little less alone in the retirement decision-making fog, I would be grateful if you left an honest review. No pressure. No gold star. Just a small kindness that helps the book reach the next tired person standing at the edge of the big decision.

Scan the QR code to visit the Amazon Review page.

References

1. Wang, M., & Shi, J. (2014). Psychological research on retirement. Annual Review of Psychology, 65, 209–233. https://doi.org/10.1146/annurev-psych-010213-115131.

2. Wang, M., Henkens, K., & van Solinge, H. (2011). Retirement adjustment: A review of theoretical and empirical advancements. American Psychologist, 66(3), 204–213. https://doi.org/10.1037/a0022414.

3. Hansson, I., Buratti, S., Thorvaldsson, V., Johansson, B., & Berg, A. I. (2018). Changes in life satisfaction in the retirement transition: Interaction effects of transition type and individual resources. Work, Aging and Retirement, 4(4), 352–366. https://doi.org/10.1093/workar/wax025.

4. La Rue, C. J., Haslam, C., & Steffens, N. K. (2022). A meta-analysis of retirement adjustment predictors. Journal of Vocational Behavior, 136, Article 103723. https://doi.org/10.1016/j.jvb.2022.103723.

5. Baumeister, R.F., Bratslavsky, E., Muraven, M., and D.M. Tice. (2018). Ego depletion: Is the active self a limited resource? Journal of Personality and Social Psychology 74(5): 1252-1265. https://assets.aclu.org/live/uploads/document/foia/1998-Journal-of-Personality-and-Social-Psychology-Ego-Depletion-Is-the-Active-Self-a-Limited-Resource.pdf.

6. Sasaki, F. (2021). Hello, Habits. A Minimalist's Guide to a Better Life. W.W. Norton and Company: New York, p.23.

7. Australian Psychological Society. (2024). How to prevent and overcome burnout. Community Resource (13 Sept 2024). https://psychology.org.au/getmedia/85f586e3-a856-47f2-a306-d0568e318193/aps-burnout-community-resource.pdf.

8. Mayo Clinic. (2023, August 10). Stress symptoms: Effects on your body and

behavior. https://www.mayoclinic.org/healthy-lifestyle/stress-management/in-depth/stress-symptoms/art-20050987.

9. Maslach, C., & Leiter, M. P. (2016). Understanding the burnout experience: Recent research and its implications for psychiatry. World Psychiatry, 15(2), 103–111. https://doi.org/10.1002/wps.20311.

10. World Health Organization. (2019). Burn-out an "occupational phenomenon": International Classification of Diseases (11th Revision). 28 May 2019. https://www.who.int/news/item/28-05-2019-burn-out-an-occupational-phenomenon-international-classification-2016of-diseases. |

11. Reijseger, G., Schaufeli, W. B., Peeters, M. C. W., Taris, T. W., van Beek, I., & Ouweneel, E. (2013). Watching the paint dry at work: Psychometric examination of the Dutch Boredom Scale. Anxiety, Stress & Coping, 26(5), 508–525. https://doi.org/10.1080/10615806.2012.720676.

12. Kivimäki, M., Nyberg, S. T., Batty, G. D., Fransson, E. I., Heikkilä, K., Alfredsson, L., ... & Theorell, T. (2012). Job strain as a risk factor for coronary heart disease: A collaborative meta-analysis of individual participant data. The Lancet, 380(9852), 1491–1497. https://doi.org/10.1016/S0140-6736(12)60994-5.

13. Ebaugh, H. R. (1988). Becoming an Ex: The Process of Role Exit. University of Chicago Press.

14. Schlossberg, N. K. (2009). Revitalizing Retirement: Reshaping Your Identity, Relationships, and Purpose. American Psychological Association.

15. Zhai L, Wang J, Liu Y and Zhang H. (2022). Involuntary retirement and depression among adults: A systematic review and meta-analysis of longitudinal studies. Frontiers in Psychiatry, 13, Article 747334. https://doi.org/10.3389/fpsyt.2022.747334.

16. Australian Securities and Investments Commission [ASIC]a. (n.d.). Work out how much you need to retire. Moneysmart. https://moneysmart.gov.au/plan-for-your-retirement/work-out-how-much-you-need-to-retire.

17. MoneyHelper. (2022). Work out how much you will need in retire-

ment. https://www.moneyhelper.org.uk/content/dam/maps/en/pensions/moneyhelper-retirement-budgeting-leaflet.pdf.

18. Australian Securities and Investments Commission [ASIC]b. (n.d.). Manage health costs in retirement. Moneysmart. https://moneysmart.gov.au/manage-your-money-in-retirement/manage-health-costs-in-retirement.

19. Australian Securities and Investments Commission [ASIC]c. (n.d.). Save for an emergency fund. Moneysmart. https://moneysmart.gov.au/saving/save-for-an-emergency-fund.

20. Australian Securities and Investments Commission [ASIC]d. (n.d.). Financial advice. Moneysmart. https://moneysmart.gov.au/financial-advice.

21. Bordia, P., Read, S., & Bordia, S. (2020). Retiring: Role identity processes in retirement transition. Journal of Organizational Behavior, 41(5), 445–460. https://doi.org/10.1002/job.2438.

22. Wang, M. (2007). Profiling retirees in the retirement transition and adjustment process: Examining the longitudinal change patterns of retirees' psychological well-being. Journal of Applied Psychology, 92(2), 455–474. https://doi.org/10.1037/0021-9010.92.2.455

23. Stryker, S., & Burke, P. J. (2000). The past, present, and future of an identity theory. Social Psychology Quarterly, 63(4), 284–297. https://doi.org/10.2307/2695840

24. Horn, A. B., Holzgang, S. A., & Rosenberger, V. (2021). Adjustment of couples to the transition to retirement: The interplay of intra- and interpersonal emotion regulation in daily life. Frontiers in Psychology, 12, Article 654255. https://doi.org/10.3389/fpsyg.2021.654255

25. Unger, D., & Potočnik, K. (2025). Happily ever after: The self- and dyadic-regulation model of retiree subjective well-being in romantic couples. Work, Aging and Retirement, waaf017. https://doi.org/10.1093/workar/waaf017

26. Chen, P., Liang, H., Zhou, Y., Zhu, G., Peng, Y., & Yao, J. (2025). The impact of spousal retirement on health: An empirical analysis based on CFPS. Frontiers in

Medicine, 11, Article 1518936. https://doi.org/10.3389/fmed.2024.1518936

27. van Solinge, H., & Henkens, K. (2005). Couples' adjustment to retirement: A multi-actor panel study. The Journals of Gerontology: Series B: Psychological Sciences and Social Sciences, 60(1), S11-S20. https://doi.org/10.1093/geronb/60.1.S11.

28. Bosma, J. J. A., Henkens, K., & van Solinge, H. (2025). The differential impact of retirement on contact frequency with family, friends, neighbors, and coworkers. The Journals of Gerontology: Series B: Psychological Sciences and Social Sciences, 80(6), gbaf042. https://doi.org/10.1093/geronb/gbaf042.

29. Kauppi, M., Virtanen, M., Pentti, J., Aalto, V., Kivimäki, M., Vahtera, J., & Stenholm, S. (2021). Social network ties before and after retirement: A cohort study. European Journal of Ageing, 18, 503–512. https://doi.org/10.1007/s10433-021-00604-y.

30. Australian Securities and Investments Commission [ASIC]. (2026, April 9). Retirement planning checklist. Moneysmart. https://static.moneysmart.gov.au/ms2026/campaign/retirement/Retirement-planning-checklist.pdf.

31. van Solinge, H., Damman, M., & Hershey, D. A. (2021). Adaptation or exploration? Understanding older workers' plans for post-retirement paid and volunteer work. Work, Aging and Retirement, 7(2), 129–142. https://doi.org/10.1093/workar/waaa027.

32. MoneyHelper. (n.d.). How to plan for retirement: Retirement planning checklist. https://www.moneyhelper.org.uk/en/pensions-and-retirement/taking-your-pension/checklist-things-to-do-as-retirement-approaches.

33. Social Security Administration. (2022, January). Your retirement checklist (Publication No. 05-10377). https://www.ssa.gov/pubs/EN-05-10377.pdf.

34. U.S. Department of Labor, Employee Benefits Security Administration. (2024). Retirement toolkit. https://www.dol.gov/sites/dolgov/files/ebsa/about-ebsa/our-activities/resource-center/publications/retirement-toolkit.pdf.

35. Australian Securities and Investments Commission [ASIC]e. (n.d.). Wills and

powers of attorney. Moneysmart. https://moneysmart.gov.au/plan-for-your-retirement/wills-and-powers-of-attorney.

36. Crary, M., Hall, D. T., Kram, K. E., Amabile, T. M., & Bailyn, L. (2025). Transitioning into retirement: The interplay of self and life structure. Work, Aging and Retirement, 11(2), 175–196. https://doi.org/10.1093/workar/waae003.

37. Wood, R. E., & Pachana, N. A. (2025). The role of meaning in the retirement transition: Scoping review. The Gerontologist, 65(6), gnaf076. https://doi.org/10.1093/geront/gnaf076.

38. La Rue, C. J., Haslam, C., Bentley, S. V., Lam, B. C. P., Steffens, N. K., Branscombe, N. R., Haslam, S. A., & Cruwys, T. (2023). GROUPS 4 RETIREMENT: A new intervention that supports well-being in the lead-up to retirement by targeting social identity management. Journal of Occupational and Organizational Psychology, 97(1), 1-26. https://doi.org/10.1111/joop.12458.

39. Fadeeva, A., Simmons, J., Thomas, L. B., Baker, K., & Ling, F. C. M. (2025). Retirement adjustment framework: Understanding the interplay between individual and contextual factors. Journal of Prevention and Health Promotion, 6(2), 335-361. https://doi.org/10.1177/26320770241279737.

40. Australian Government. (2020). Retirement Income Review: Final report. Treasury. https://treasury.gov.au/publication/p2020-100554.

41. Coates, B., Moloney, J., and Suckling, E. (2025). Simpler super: Taking the stress out of retirement. Grattan Institute. https://grattan.edu.au/wp-content/uploads/2025/01/Simpler-Super-Grattan-Institute-Report.pdf.

www.ingramcontent.com/pod-product-compliance
Lightning Source LLC
LaVergne TN
LVHW022101200926
848481LV00003B/1017